A Woman's Book of Power

Also by Karen Andes

A Woman's Book of Strength

A Woman's Book of Power

Using Dance to Cultivate Energy and
Health in Mind, Body, and Spirit

Karen Andes

A PERIGEE BOOK

A Perigee Book
Published by The Berkley Publishing Group
A member of Penguin Putnam Inc.
200 Madison Avenue
New York, NY 10016

First edition: January 1998

Published simultaneously in Canada.

The Putnam Berkley World Wide Web site address is
http://www.berkley.com

Library of Congress Cataloging-in Publication Data
Andes, Karen
A woman's book of power : using dance to cultivate energy and health in mind,
body, and spirit / Karen Andes. — 1st ed.
p.   cm.
"A Perigee book."
Includes bibliographical references
ISBN 0-399-52372-3
1. Exercise for women—Psychological aspects.   2. Feminist theory.   3.
Dance—Psychological aspects.   4. Movement education.   I. Title.
GV482.A53   1998
613.7'045—DC21   97-23333
                                                                  CIP

Printed in the United States of America

10   9   8   7   6   5   4   3   2   1

*This book is dedicated to all of you in whom the Feminine Divine
at first slumbers, rustles, wakes,
later whispers, guides and corrects
and finally sings, howls and informs your every move.
The Goddess reminds you to find your dance and dance it.*

Contents

PART TWO

Body and Shapes

PART THREE

Mind and Future

Acknowledgments

I've discovered that I can't just write books. I have to live them. Living this book has taken me not only into my own past, present and future but through all time and into other people's pasts, lives and dreams as well.

My thanks to all the people I have met along the way who've been moved beyond reason to dig for sacred treasure in themselves. They have given me the courage to put this work out in the world so the circle can grow wider.

My special thanks to:

my sister Elizabeth Andes Bell, who got me dancing before I could walk,

my father, Charles Andes, who showed me that power must be anchored in the spirit before it can bloom in the world,

my mother-in-law, Yelba Nunez, who sustained us with prayers and food,

my agent, Julie Merberg, who maintained her belief in this project from the start, even when I didn't know where it was leading,

my editor, Sheila Curry, who accepted the unusual unfolding of this book with an open mind.

My thanks to all the dance teachers out there who continue to give their heart and sweat and never earn enough for their efforts, especially:

Carolena Nericcio of FatChanceBellyDance in San Francisco—for sharing her artistic sensibilities, curiosity and intelligence.

Sherry Brier of Inner Rhythm in Mill Valley, California—for being the first one to ferry me into the mystical world of shimmies, shakes and body rolls.

Terry Sendgraff of Motivity, in Oakland, California—for her generous spirit and for showing me how a great teacher should be.

My thanks to all the dancers and athletes who thrilled and inspired me to keep moving and searching . . . all the writers, some of whom I've met, many I haven't, whose books informed my own . . . and the artists throughout antiquity who captured the essence of dance and spirit who've helped us all learn from our past.

My extreme thanks to my husband, Martine, who lovingly understood my need to dance even when he was digging in the mud and building our house. Although there were times when our worlds seemed very far apart, we were both led by the same instincts—to round off the hard edges and create shapes, textures and colors that raise the spirit.

Once again, my greatest thanks to my invisible collaborator—the voice that comes in the dark. Thanks for your visits and for guiding me, despite my resistance and fear of being "found out," so deep into the history of women and so deep into myself. You remind me that my journey, however individual, is but a symbol for the journey of all women.

Blessings be.

A Woman's
Book of Power

The author, at age four,
first discovers her Divine Feminine

After many years, the author,
age forty, finds Her again.

Introduction:
Why I Had to Write This Book

"What happened in India, I came to understand, was that I had experienced myself as sexual, sacred and powerful in a way no modern woman in the West can. Our psychological being has been severed from our biological selves for so long that we are completely cut off from our true natures. Because I was in touch with this strength, with the celebration and fullness of my being for even so limited a time, I could never return to my old ways of seeing the world . . . My erotic self, the deep life force within, had been activated and there was no way to put the genie back in the bottle."

—ELINOR GADON, *The Once and Future Goddess*

At the time I began writing this book, my feminine spirit coiled up out of the dark, murky waters of my unconscious and started rattling my cage, saying "own me!" This was a voluptuous, articulate, powerful and *sacred* part of my personality that suddenly demanded to be born, fully formed, like Athena from the head of Zeus. At first, this seemed like a new dimension of my female-ness. Up until then, I had adopted a soft androgyny as a way to camouflage feminine "weakness" and therefore get ahead in the world. I had three black leather jackets and not much respect for froo-froo and lace or anything else that screamed "helpless!" I did not equate softness with "power." I soon came to realize, however, that my volcanically erupting femininity wasn't at all weak or powerless. It wasn't even a new side of my nature at all, but an ancient and primordial one, a potent, precious, fully blossomed sexuality that bore no resemblance to the feminine sexuality I saw portrayed in movies or on television. This had a spiritual dimension and depth that both moved and frightened me, and I wasn't sure what it meant or what to do with it.

For a while I didn't respond except to buy myself some lingerie. Becoming ultrafeminine wasn't practical in my life. I didn't think of myself as a "high maintenance" female; I didn't paint my nails or wear high heels. I had a consulting job with a corporation for which I traveled, wore a suit and carried a briefcase. I also worked as a personal trainer, carried a clipboard and led my clients through the masculine maze of modern gyms. At home I helped my husband reconstruct our house, wore overalls and occasionally dug trenches or worked with power tools. When I could carve time for myself, I put on sweats, lifted weights and went running in the hills. I did not need a primitive wild woman, wearing satin and feathers, eating into my day. I needed to pay my bills, stay in shape and heed my ambition. To achieve this, I thought I needed to edit who I was. I didn't have much time for "whimsy." These things didn't help me survive or serve my professional image. It seemed more useful to become a warrior, a "mini man," complete with muscles. So for a while, I continued to ignore the rumblings and focused only on those things that served my income or career.

It didn't take long to become both depressed and ill. Once I'd become aware of the potent, playful side of my feminine spirit, I couldn't continue to ignore it. It wanted to come out, dress up and play. But how? Where? When could I schedule it in? How was I supposed to be? I went through a long period of confusion, no longer fitting into my old self and not yet born into the new. I heard people speak of "personal power," "owning power" and "giving away power" but I really had no idea what they meant. I didn't seem to have power in the outside world and didn't know how to tap the power within. I seemed to be in a spiritual apogee, with all signals down, all contact lost with the Mother Ship. Sometimes I just sat and cried. I didn't see, as I so clearly do now, what was wrong. I couldn't ignore the Divine Feminine!

Illness and depression served to soften my edges so I could hear the voice inside, which told me to forget about being tough for a while and create a sanctuary so this loopy, sensual wild woman could break out of her cage. If I didn't, something inside me would wither and die. I still didn't know what to *do*. But I realized this wasn't about "doing"; this was about "being" and allowing the messages to come—very difficult concepts for an ambitious person. So I prayed and in the midst of the fog came two shining words: "belly dance." Belly dance? Now here was something entirely irrational.

Like many people, I had a stereotypical image of belly dance as something performed by large women in sequins and pink chiffon. I thought of it as a cheap nightclub act rather than a legitimate form of exercise, art or entertainment. Belly dancing certainly wasn't in line with my fitness background, where every action must serve a logical purpose. Nor did it jive with the physical ideal of a strong, muscular body that I myself not only valued but had achieved. It didn't fit my idea of artistic expression either because in the worlds of ballet, modern dance and jazz, belly dance never factored in as real "dance." But something about it called to me *because* it seemed frivolous and served none of my rational needs. I could wear veils if I wanted to and dance in circles. It sounded like good therapy. I signed up for class.

The soft, rounded movements gave my feminine spirit an immediate sense of freedom. As soon as I started dancing, something familiar inside woke up—me! Where had I been all these years and why hadn't I kept dancing? When I was a little girl, my favorite thing in the world had been playing dress-up and dancing around the room. Now I was forty and doing the same thing—only it was better and more fun and I was a much better dancer. Maybe it was a bizarre form of therapy, but it was simple and it worked.

Because I had loved dancing as a child, I'd wanted to *be* a dancer. But then, in my twenties I moved to New York, struggled in highly competitive dance classes, felt humiliated in auditions and got a taste of the hard dancer's life. These things effectively wiped out the pure pleasure I'd found in dance. I'd also never found a style that felt right for me. Ballet seemed too fussy and discriminating, jazz too glitzy, modern too intense, ethnic too alien and aerobics too rigid—and nothing about aerobics music ever inspired me. I also didn't like having to move according to someone else's rules. For many years I channeled my moving spirit into "fitness," although I'd still hear a good song and break into spontaneous dancing. When I finally I started belly dancing, I discovered that I could use the soft basic motions to feel that joy again and create my *own* dance—one that served *my* body, *my* ability and provided just the right balance of exercise and self-expression—on my terms and not someone else's. At forty years old, just the age when dancers used to hang up their leotards for good, I seemed to have found my dance and gave myself permission to dance it. I did not stay with pure belly dance technique for long but let it evolve into a universal collection of spirals, curves and wavy lines. (My style seems to be a mishmash of cultures.) Yet these shapes let me tap a creative, infinite source that seemed to have been waiting inside for years. All I had to do was start dancing and out it would pour. After just a few months, I was changed. The world had become richer. Flavors, textures, colors, rhythms, feelings all moved me more deeply, and my ability to sense and express was stronger than ever before.

I began to wonder: If I harbored such a secret dancer within, eagerly waiting for permission to come out, how many other women did as well? If I'd gotten ill from sporting too much "male energy," how many other achievement-oriented women were suffering from a similar ailment? And what of the women who had too *much* femininity, but in a meek, fearful manner—one that lacked balance and a sensual, sacred power? It seemed that finding a sanctuary for a power that is feminine, sensual and seemingly infinite was something that could help us all. I started to dance because of me. But I soon felt that I was dancing for all women.

I also began to have the sensation while I was dancing that my ancestors were waking up inside me—and not just the ones who could be traced on a family tree. My roots are mostly Celtic. But I'd hear the same strains of pipe, fiddle and drum floating as naturally through a Celtic song as one from the Middle East, India, Africa or Spain—and I would be moved to tears. I realized that I was the product of thousands of years of tribes wandering across Europe, Asia, the Middle East, Africa, the Americas. My roots no longer seemed to be just Celtic anymore, but Moorish, Egyptian, Gypsy and who knows what else. The deeper I looked into the past, the more I saw that despite our lines of cultural distinction, we are but one family. We have shared, borrowed and stolen traditions, icons, artwork, architecture, religions, myths, deities, saints, remedies, recipes, melodies, rhythms and dances. Thus, I felt drawn to honor my *human* heritage, and especially the heritage of women, through the vehicle of expression that defies language and time—dance!

I was inspired to study everything I could about the history of dance and its sacred dimension. This was not an easy task since so little tangible information exists, with almost nothing written down. Dance is, after all, the most ephemeral of the arts. Plus, it's difficult to extract pure sacred dance from secular or seductive dance, especially when many of the same moves, the hip motions of belly dance, for instance, were probably used just as often during sacred rituals as in smoky nightclubs. It was my intention, therefore, not to search out the *choreography* of dances that may have been used in ritual celebrations but, more important, the *essence* of whatever it is that makes movement sacred to begin with. I wanted to use that essence to transport myself to an expanded, ecstatic state—and, if possible, identify whatever took me there so I could help others do the same.

My studies took me into all sorts of classes, dance festivals and arts libraries (there aren't many books on ancient, sacred dance, however). If I'd had enough money and time I'd have traveled around the world and hired a psychic to "channel" long-dead dancers. But I grabbed any information— not only about Middle Eastern dance but also the Hula, Indian temple dances, Flamenco, various forms of African, Haitian and Cuban dance and folk dances from Ireland, Scotland, North, South and Central America— from any source I could find. I searched for consistencies, truths, any connecting threads that revealed something important about humans and dance.

What seemed to make dance (or any action, object or place) sacred was the power we assigned to it. We used it to transport ourselves into an "altered" state, a heightened appreciation of even the most subtle gestures. While dancing, we welcomed an invisible "other" force—love, God, an "energy," magic, power or whatever you choose to call it so that the dance seemed to pass through like a breeze or a visitation from the angels. If there was technique involved, at some point we had to cut ourselves loose from it and simply let ourselves be danced.

The shapes we made with our bodies also seemed to have some impact on how the dance affected us. Most of the dance forms I studied contained at least one of four basic shapes: circles, figure 8's, spirals and snaking undulations—soft, rounded shapes. Many contained hard, "masculine" lines as well, for punctuation and dramatic flare but most were dominated by the round, the feminine. This came as no surprise since these are the natural shapes our bodies create when we're freely, unself-consciously dancing. We spin, spiral, wave around. These shapes are *the* raw material of organic movement and have the power to flow without interruption, even for hours at a time. They are powerful, but not in an obvious way like a punch or kick. They are also gentle on the body, yet their effects on our muscles and spirits can be profound. Although their power becomes greater with practice, they can provide an immediate opening into an authentic side of the self.

The four shapes are common in the natural world. They appear around us everywhere: in the ripples of water, the perfect symmetry of an open clam shell, the spiraling growth of plants, an undulating wave. They also appear in the microscopic world of cells, the subatomic world of particles and waves. Even the planets sketch such patterns as they move through space. Although it sounds corny, when we draw such shapes with our movements, we are in harmony with the world around us.

Not surprisingly, these shapes have earned a place of reverence throughout history. These symbols spanned continents, cultures and centuries. Nearly every major civilization created artwork that featured spirals, meandering, interlocking snakes and circles (also other "sacred" geometric forms like the triangle, cross, five- and six-pointed stars) as if these shapes were mini maps to the mysteries of the universe. The four dancing shapes were particularly important in ancient *matriarchal* societies which existed in ancient Egypt, Crete, Old Europe, India and other places where people worshiped Mother Earth, a Mother God or "the Goddess." People from these cultures believed that a feminine divine force was responsible for all cycles of life, death and rebirth. Because these four gentle shapes were self-contained or flowed back on themselves, they seemed to represent all that is yielding, enduring, enveloping, receptive, infinite and therefore powerfully feminine. These shapes have endured and continue to move, inspire and seduce us.

I will touch more deeply on the Goddess connection to dance and our own personal evolutions in part 1. For now, suffice it to say that in these ancient cultures, women's bodies were considered sacred because they represented the Goddess in miniature. Historians believe that women in these times not only used dance as an offering to the Goddess but as a way to *be* Her or a part of Her. From the perspective of later religions in which we viewed ourselves as separate from God (and a male God at that), this no doubt seemed both presumptuous and obscene.

However, the more I studied the Goddess, the more I realized that the spirit of ancient, sacred dancing was what I was after. I had already discovered that dance had the ability to take us both out of ourselves and into ourselves at the same time. But the connection of dance to the Goddess or a feminine spiritual power came as a huge revelation. In the Sunday schools I'd gone to, nobody ever mentioned a female God or let us get up and dance our prayers. In the dance schools I'd gone to, no one spoke of dancing a divine spirit. In high school and college, where we studied goddesses in Greek mythology and art history, we never delved very deeply into their stories. After a few intriguing lines about whatever subjects they ruled: love, the hearth and home, marriage, wisdom or the hunt, we always seemed to skip over them, as if they weren't worth our full attention, as if we had to get on to more useful subjects. There was never any talk of a womanly, mystical force or of a long-buried, feminine, sensual, spiritual history that had been smudged out throughout the centuries. So, like a lot of women, I had no choice but to delve into the subjects myself.

When I was young, I sometimes wondered if I came from some other planet. After all, I used to watch those bad sci-fi movies from the sixties with planets full of women wearing negligees and thought, "I'd like to live *there.*" But the more I learned about our spiritual history, the more I realized I wasn't from another planet. I was from the *Earth* and my yearnings for a feminine sacred power that I could honor with my body, brain and all my creative juices were normal. In fact, it was already programmed into my genetic code. I felt that I had been moving toward honoring this heritage for my entire life but had only just realized it. More profoundly, it seemed that this was true for all women. We've all been edging, through thousands of years of darkness, toward a communion (conscious or not) with the divinely feminine power inside each of us.

After examining the past, I took a close look at the present and, by comparison, the modern world looked very flat. We used to regard our female bodies as sacred. Now we're at war with them. We used to consider our hips as magic bowls of manifestation, where spirit could form into matter. Now we do whatever we can to hide, harden and "get rid" of them. We used to model ourselves on various goddesses and owned our ampleness without shame or apology. Now we model ourselves on unnatural icons: emaciated models or surgically enhanced "bionic" celebrities. We used to dance in the round, mimicking the curvy motions of Nature. Now we dance in straight lines, mimicking things man-made and militaristic, the bottom line, the shortest distance between two points. No wonder so many of us feel cut off from the Source! No wonder, too, that so few of us feel nurtured by traditional Western exercise! Somewhere along the way, we forgot to value our roundness, our snaking hips, and with that we lost touch with who we really are, forgot that honoring the body is *the* doorway into spirit. Somehow, too, we forgot that dance was an ideal way of celebrating our powerful femininity.

I still see so many unhappy modern women, dragging themselves through business and fitness routines, with their sacred beauty fast asleep, when in fact, it's this power that could provide the juice, joy, hope and enthusiasm that's missing. It's important that we *experience* ourselves as divinely, profoundly and potently feminine because we are sensual creatures. We can't just think about it; we must taste it, feel it, sing and dance it before we can take it with us into all parts of our lives. We also need to know who we were, so we can better know who we are and who we can become. We *can* own this part of ourselves without having to live in a cave. We can express the power in subtle ways, own it and still have jobs, families and live in "the real world."

Dance provides an easy way to contact and express our spirits—and it's a great workout. I believe most women are natural dancers. Regardless of our experience or level of technique, we all understand the concept of "flow," which is the essence of dance. Learning how to dance our spirits is at least partly a matter of tapping the rhythms and dances that are already within. We don't need years of technique to enjoy this. We don't need to "be good at it." We don't even need to share any interest in the "Goddess" to gain benefits from moving this way. Most of us probably already know how to dance our spirits, but many of us have forgotten how.

I know it's hard to learn how to dance from a book. However, I took that into consideration when I created the exercises presented here. The idea is not to learn specific choreography but a very simple, visual *formula,* which can help each of us find our *own* dances. The formula is basic enough for "nondancers," yet rich enough for those with years of training. Its influences come not only from "belly" dance but from other forms of dance, martial arts, fitness and yoga. I originally created this approach for me because I wanted movement that would feed my soul while keeping me lean and fit. I get easily bored on treadmills and stair machines. But with good music, I can dance for an hour and not realize the time has passed. It has since become my driving passion to share dance with women of all ages and ability because I know there's value here for all, both sacred and secular.

By now you've probably realized this is not your typical exercise book. You will find no six-week program, no list of guarantees and surefire benefits, no supermodels or celebrities who know nothing about fitness yet are blessed with good genes, plastic surgeons and speedy metabolisms telling you how to look like them. The objective of the dance presented here is not to burn calories and fat (although it does), turn certain soft body parts into sheets of steel (although it can), give you impressive endurance (although it can do that, too), prevent arthritis (actually, dance is great for loosening up tight joints—one key to enhanced longevity), help you look younger (although looking radiant, graceful and happy makes you ageless) or improve your sex life (yet, this wasn't a fertility dance for nothing). The real objective is to take something as mundane as a workout and turn it into an act of celebration so you can taste your joy.

The power of the feminine has added a sense of humor, justice, and potent sensuality to my movements and life in general. I'm spoiled now and can no longer settle only for linear workouts or anything else that's missing this magic touch. I believe it is the spirit of the feminine that informed this book and the dance presented here. It's certainly Her spirit that pours out of me when I dance. I also believe that it is the power of the feminine spirit which is sorely absent from the world—not just in women's lives but in men's lives, too. If we generate this spirit in ourselves, it will ripple out. When there are enough of us, we'll be a powerful force to contend with and the divine feminine spirit will once again be restored to a place of respect. I believe we're on our way. This spirit has become my key to wholeness. I hope it will become yours.

PART ONE

Spirit and Sex

1 The Dance of Power

This book is about a type of power and a style of dance that draw from a "divine," feminine source. The power I speak of is subtle, energetic and throbs in every organic thing. The dance I address is fluid, spontaneous, expressive.

Although dance and power may not seem related, the same spirit can drive them. Both require balance, discipline, strength, courage and skill to practice with integrity. Both lend us elegance, longevity and enthusiasm. But both the words "power" and "dance" can be intimidating, as well. Many of us may long to dance but don't think of ourselves as "dancers," are afraid to look foolish and find dance steps too difficult. Those of us who actually become "dancers" often worry that age or disability will diminish our grace. Many of us may also long for power so we can put our thoughts, feelings and visions out in the world, yet we're afraid to fail or don't want to become oppressive like others in power. Those of us who actually become "powerful," at least in the outside world, often worry that someone younger, more charismatic and more able will snatch our influence. There is, however, a dance of power and a powerful sort of *dancing* that can sustain us all our lives—as long as we put them into practice.

Power is defined in the dictionary as: "authority, capacity, effectiveness, control, control *over*, force, speed and energy." But there is also a more esoteric definition that doesn't appear in most dictionaries. There is a greater power, an "immanence" or godlike force that exists within, a mysterious, magnificent pulsing which has been called all kinds of names—"chi," "prana," "life force," "soul"—that we all possess. This power becomes most evident not when we practice control *over*, or use our will, ego or brute force to achieve a goal, but when we surrender those things, so a more profound power can flow through.

Dancing could also be defined the same way. It, too, requires "authority, capacity, effectiveness, control, control *over*, force, speed and energy." Yet, for a dance to resonate with meaning and emotion, move the dancer, the audience and rise above simple calisthenics, there must also be a surrender of ego or outcome, so the power can flow through. If there is choreography to be followed, it must serve only a supporting role. The idea is to let the full presence of the dancer be the star. What is most impressive about a dancer or a dance is not the movement but the human spirit in motion. When we clear away the obstacles, every one of us can tap this power so it flows from our movements, our voices, our imaginations, or the way we interact with others in the world. It is a power, which once tapped, seems to dance on its own.

"Feminine power" has long been associated with the dark, feeling side of human nature. Throughout history it has been undervalued, dishonored and almost destroyed. It, too, has been called all kinds of names: women's intuition, old wives' tales, superstition, a witch's brew, magic, possession, foolishness. It seems to have little in common with the "masculine" traits people associate with "power." But it is slowly moving back into people's awareness. Many are realizing that it is the quality of our *presence* and our internal worlds that determine whether we're happy and not just our accomplishments, trophies, salaries or physiques. When we are powered at least in part by the sacred aspect of the feminine, we don't operate only out of self-interest. There's another force instructing us. Consequently, we become more fearless, more willing to take risks or fail, more willing to encourage others or dance just for the pleasure of it.

Feminine power has little in common with the "masculine" power of armies, governments or corporations which have been famous for obliterating resources, cultures and claiming the spoils as their own. Feminine power is also nothing like the simple force of a power lifter. *That* sort of power is goal oriented, efficient and can be broken down into a scientific formula. Feminine power is rarely efficient and can almost never be broken down into a formula. It *is* seemingly mysterious. It represents, perhaps, the place where dances, life, ideas, inspirations and justice come *from*. It's not logical and yet there's an order about it, a symmetrical, cyclical pattern that it seems to follow. In its purest state, feminine power is about allowing, enjoying, evolving and letting everyone be a winner. It's artistic, kindhearted, peace loving and nurturing, and that's one reason why it's been so easy to destroy.

Women aren't the only ones who possess feminine power—just as men aren't the only ones who long to dominate or control—and no one, I believe, possesses either feminine or masculine power in their unadulterated forms. "Feminine" power has associations with the female because it is in line with the feminine principle, the yin, the soft, the flowing. Contrary to what some may think, it doesn't represent our weaker side but one that is *more* powerful. It seems to be much bigger than our individual desires. It doesn't force itself on anyone. It just is.

Dancing in a way that is easy, natural and not self-conscious lets us manifest this power in a physical way. But dance only puts us in touch with this power when we dance to please *ourselves*, take the opportunity to listen, feel, play and be fully present. It doesn't come when we get stuck in the choreography, dance for approval or to shrink our thighs.

The curving shapes I present here are useful tools for accessing this feminine power because they provide a stepping-off point into a spontaneous, playful sort of movement that each of us can interpret so it feels natural to our bodies and abilities. These shapes already exist in our dances. Perhaps I am simply identifying what others may find obvious; however, these patterns represent the flowing power of the feminine. They also complement our womanly bodies and put us in harmony with ourselves and Nature. For those of us who have at one time waged war against our bodies in fitness or dance regimens, this is a ticket to freedom and self-delight. Let me be very clear about this. The purpose of accessing feminine power through movement is to experience joy—not only the joy that comes from being lighthearted and happy but also the joy that comes from being genuine.

"Feminine" power is physical, sensual, sexual. We don't *think* our power; we feel it. It also happens to grow directly out of our hips, buttocks, bellies and thighs. How ironic that the area we most loathe on our bodies and try to "tame" with diets and exercise is actually *the root of our greatest power.* This is why I believe dancing holds an important place in our development as powerful women because it can help us experience the power we're already sitting on. There's perhaps no greater celebration of the female body

"Women experience power as rooted in their biological selves, an enabling life force in contrast to the authoritative, hierarchical 'power over . . .'"

—Elinor Gadon, *The Once and Future Goddess*

than to swivel, bump and grind our hips, and even, Heaven forbid, *shake our fat!* When we do this our once poor, beleaguered hip-buttock-thigh area sends out an immediate cry of relief, and years of shame, numbness and armor start to melt away. When we stop scrutinizing our bodies for every little flaw, we begin to own the power of our femininity and learn to dance with what we have. This is power with no apologies.

Once we have accessed this power through movement, we can begin to use it in other places where we "dance" through life, especially at work and in relationships. The world, after all, doesn't exactly encourage feminine power and a woman who openly embraces it can easily be viewed as odd or a threat. Feminine sacred power is still considered "esoteric," which means "intended for the few." Except in friendly circles, it's often much easier to keep such power behind a veil.

More women than ever have been coming into positions of secular power. But there are many who come to it incomplete, unaware of our gender's rich, buried history with sacred power. Many of us have imitated "male" power because we thought that's what power was and how it should be exercised. We've done a good job of it, too. We've learned how to speak in numbers, work deals on the golf course, drink martinis and smoke cigars. We've also learned how to bench-press, throw a ball and run with the best of them. But opening up to our feminine power could give us a grounding confidence to practice worldly power with a full sense of who we are.

Many of us have already started feeling the Divine Feminine rattling our cages. We've been quitting our jobs or working "flex time" to spend more time with our children, families, friends, ourselves. We've been joining women's groups, fixing up our houses, painting, singing or dancing for the first time in years—or ever. We're realizing that our souls have been craving more nourishment and that the power that grows from the feminine feeds our souls in a way that male power does not. Outward success only sustains us when it's mixed with a substance that grows from our guts. Otherwise it fades as fast as a sugar high.

It's no surprise that many women who've come into positions of secular power have been like starved prisoners at a feast. We *have* been starved of our power. It's been floundering in the shadows. Until recently, few of us even knew what it was and we're still defining it. Unfortunately, there are still many of us who don't even know it exists. We've probably all met some women in power who order people around just as others did them—

"The development of our power comes from daily practices that strengthen our bodies, psyches and souls."

—HALLIE AUSTEN IGLEHART, *Womanspirit, A Guide to Woman's Wisdom*

"Ours is a search for meaning, for that which has been lost and for what can be recovered . . . Until women can visualize the sacred female, they cannot be whole and society cannot be whole."

—ELINOR GADON, *The Once and Future Goddess*

women who changed from victim to abuser with a vengeance. This isn't power; it's fear. Often, their worst nightmare is that someone younger, more beautiful and cunning will take their place. The truth is, somebody eventually does. The question is, What do we do so *we* don't end up like that? The only answer is "Stoke the sacred fire."

We *must* have safe havens where we can cultivate our authenticity, be raw, unedited, beautiful, ugly, angry, happy, depressed, weary, vivacious, peaceful, sensual, mature, full of wisdom and possess a youthful sense of play. We need to discuss and display this sacred power openly among ourselves instead of keeping it secret because unexpressed, our power turns into anger, depression or fear. Like anything else, if we don't use it, we lose it. There are countless ways to "use it." Dancing together (or alone in our living rooms yet linked by our interests) is one very simple way to keep the sacred fires burning.

The key to our power is feeling. When we fearlessly own the full spectrum of our emotions (which also serves all our creations) we begin to own the truth of who we are. Sometimes to discover this, we have to descend to our depths to repair old wounds or unearth old desires. But out of the old pieces and the new we form a new creation—our lives. The results of such work are always positive even if some of the steps we take to achieve them cause pain. But that pain is short-term. The pain of never owning our full, rich, authentic selves lasts forever.

On the one hand, to come into power simply through business, faith or some other means while ignoring the body is to experience an energy that doesn't spring from anywhere. On the other hand, to create a powerful body while ignoring the spirit makes an attractive but empty working shell, with its movements geared more for attention, prizes and vanity than knowledge of the self. But when the body and spirit are linked (not just the body and mind—but the feminine body's deep, gutsy, raucous, sexy soul!), the lights go on and stay on—or at least we know how to find the switch. Connecting the mind, body and soul is great fun and creates a high level of health!

We are all powerful women at heart. We are all natural dancers, too. The opportunity to experience our sacred, dancing power comes up many times, in spiral fashion, throughout our lives. It's natural to "lose it" from time to time. We all get pulled into various traps, forget who we are, surrender to our fears, try to control all those things that refuse to be controlled or damn ourselves for not being perfect. The mantle of sacred power, however, is always there waiting to comfort us, just as the dance is

"This power—the same energy that may now manifest as hostility, envy, hatred, rage, bitterness, self-pity or blame—can become a creative power to build happiness, pleasure, love, expansion, for yourself and others around you."

—EVA PIERRAKOS,
The Pathwork of Self-Transformation

"Whatever is flexible and flowing will tend to grow, whatever is rigid and blocked will wither and die."

—*Tao Te Ching*

always waiting to be danced. It's that simple. When we believe it, we make it so. When we go to the temple to dance, the dances come. The more we call on our power, the more we understand that, in fact, we control more than we realize and are perfect just as we are.

The Difference Between Strength and Power

In my first book, *A Woman's Book of Strength*, I wrote about the importance of physical strength for women and how it serves both the body and sense of self. In this book, I'm doing the same with power. The words *strength* and *power* are often used interchangeably, especially when describing movement or business. But they really aren't the same.

Strength is the foundation, the stem in our evolution as whole, mature beings. Power is the next phase, the bloom on the rose. Strength requires an almost static state. It gives the ability to endure, exert effort, sit in discomfort or move with an obdurate self-assurance. Power takes strength and builds on it, adds speed, direction, energy, the ability to get things done, move, dance, fly. Although strength and power borrow from each other, compete with each other and are often confused like twins, they're also separate with individual personalities. Strength without power is beautiful to behold but leaden, stocky, slow to get the joke, a little head on a muscular frame. Power without strength is hollow and short-lived, a monstrous head on a tiny body. Power blossoming out of strength is natural. But when power comes first and strength later, the process is backwards. Strength is more like protein that builds and repairs; power is the carbohydrate that sometimes lifts the blood in a sugar high and can send it crashing down unless there's a little protein in the mix.

The language of strength is simple and serious. It has one subject, object and verb and its purpose is to overcome a single challenge. The mission of the weight lifter, for instance, is to move a weight through space with clean, repetitive motions and a singular focus. She must block out all distractions and almost hypnotize herself to complete the task. The language of power, at least power in *motion*, is playful and unpredictable. There are countless subjects, objects and verbs coming in from all directions—also adverbs, adjectives, sighs, drama, laughter. The mission of the dancer or martial artist is constantly to shift, anticipate, deflect, advance and orchestrate these things so the pieces hang together as one.

Strength is shy; power is self-assured. Strength is steady; power surges. Strength hums; power sings. Strength lets us work in a small space. Power opens up the world. Strength is the slower, plainer, younger sister, often overlooked—and perhaps the harder-working and humbler of the two. Power is quick-witted, charming, good-looking, often brash and seductive, even cunning. If it wants something, it knows how to get attention.

Although strength ought to come first and power later (so we have the strength to handle power wisely), people often go first for power for its promise of flashy rewards. Building strength takes plodding, unglamorous work, the kind of labor that isn't respected in our culture which still worships "overnight" sensations, high-rolling megabuck mergers, souped-up cars, breast implants on a body with 6 percent fat and muscles stoked on steroids. We have no modern mythology supporting slow, steady progress. We have no stories, as they do in China, of young disciples polishing the swords of the great masters for twenty years before being *allowed* to take one lesson. If we can't get it in thirty minutes twice a week, then forget it. If we can't buy it, we don't understand. We pray for lotteries, lovers and "perfect bodies" to drop out of the heavens (an awful lot to ask of the Great Mother), wanting the prize without doing the work. We marry the person we've known for just a few days, weeks or months, still aglow in Step One of a newly opened heart, without having lived through even one winter of discontent to test it for strength. Then we're devastated when problems appear.

Power may bring a rush of adrenaline and a mighty hand to wield influence over others, but only strength supplies the endurance to follow through. Without strength, power brings the fear of adversaries and critics lurking around every corner. Power that blossoms from strength, however, calms the fear; no one can take away what we own inside our skin. Even when someone pulls a coup and snatches away our power (which is highly likely), the sort of power I speak of here gives us the dignity to ride through rough cycles and total loss of power without becoming bitter and afraid.

Both strength and power can be false and true. False strength is all muscle but no tender heart. True strength is patience, persistence through resistance, compassion. False power is authority without experience, giving orders without understanding what it takes to do the work. True power comes to someone who has climbed the ladder rung by rung and asks others not to do the impossible, only to stretch their self-limiting beliefs.

Power can come to those of us who aren't ready to handle it. When it comes in a rush, bringing the thrill of the chase, the big deal and all its toys—the title, the salary, the car, the clothes, the house, the attention—it's intoxicating and oh so easy to adapt to. We want to believe it will be there forever simply because it was endowed once. But without the foundation of strength to support it, the fall from power is steep and even fatal. Like the daily cultivation of strength in muscle and in mind, power needs to be practiced consistently, humbly, earned and created over and over again.

2 A Spirit-Power of Our Own

To find the power that is innate in women, we have to go back to 25,000 or 40,000 B.C. (some historians believe 70,000 B.C.!) and work forward until approximately the birth of Christ. This was the golden era of the "Goddess," a time when people believed that a feminine, divine force controlled all cycles of birth, death and rebirth. People believed in this so strongly that even after the Christian Church and other single-male-god religions tried to wipe out everything related to the "Goddess," Her shadow-presence remained veiled in church ritual, artwork, even in the Bible. But to recognize the symbols, we have to know what to look for.

Goddess cultures existed most profoundly in Mesopotamia (what is now Iraq, Kuwait, Syria), Anatolia (in southern Turkey), Malta, also in Egypt and Arabia (what is now Lebanon). But evidence of Goddess cultures has been found all over Asia, Africa and what anthropologist Maria Gimbutas calls "Old Europe," which "extended from the Adriatic to the Aegean, including the islands, and as far north as Czechoslovakia, southern Poland and the Western Ukraine."[1] Greece, Italy, Ireland, Scotland and England, China, India and Tibet all had important and powerful goddesses within their mythology. Even the Incans, Aztecs, Mayans and American Indians revered goddesses. Goddesses were global.

[1] Elinor Gadon, *The Once and Future Goddess* (San Francisco: Harper, 1989), 40.

Nowadays when people call a woman a "goddess" they usually refer to her beauty, her maiden youth and ripe sexuality. But goddesses were much more interesting than this. They were young and "older than time." They were beautiful and hideous. They were the ultimate earth mothers who also devoured their young. They were virgins, legendary lovers, warriors, dancers, daughters, mothers, sages; also vengeful queens, given to bouts of jealousy and rage and rulers of the Underworld. They protected animals, plants, children. They also ruled wisdom, justice and higher learning. Many had even conceived and birthed themselves or were born of the sea, the Earth or sky or from a union of mortals and gods. Since they created themselves, they could re-create themselves whenever necessary. Although the power possessed by goddesses may have seemed mysterious and omnipotent, it was also earthy, tangible and part of daily life. Goddesses ruled both the visible and invisible worlds, individual lives and the universe.

In a number of different cultures, many goddesses were portrayed as "maiden, mother and crone," signifying a full life cycle. Goddesses who embodied all three phases were called "triple goddesses." What determined their passage from one cycle to the next (and a mortal woman's passage) were the blood cycles: menarche, menstruation and menopause. Goddesses were adept at being all three at once or switching back and forth when necessary, demonstrating their power of mutability and how they (and therefore we) could be all-knowing and all things at one time.

The blood cycles were holy (not a "curse"). In matriarchal cultures, menstruation used to be considered a time when a woman could rest and go into the "cave of darkness" to meditate. Bleeding monthly demonstrated that women could literally suffer a little "death wound" and emerge days later, healed, flushed clean and, like the serpent, shed of old skin, "proving" that we possessed at least one aspect of goddess power—the ability to regenerate life. Our bleeding time still begs us to pull inward, rest and reflect, but modern life rarely lets us make time for this. Bleeding no longer dictates the passages of our lives to the same extent. Just because we bleed at puberty doesn't make us fit to be mothers. Just because we stop bleeding at menopause doesn't make us crones. With longer life spans and science on our side, we're more capable of moving against the tides of biology; and with practices like dancing, exercise, prayer, learning about new things and enjoying the company of our friends, we can soften the impact of age. But the tides of blood still pull us nonetheless.

Goddesses always seemed to know exactly where they stood in their life cycles. They also seemed to be in full command of their sexuality, knew how to enjoy it and use it for other purposes. They were sexy, adventurous and kinky, even by today's standards. Artwork and mythology placed them with many lovers: sons, fathers, brothers, strangers, stags, bulls, gods, occasionally husbands and other goddesses, too. They would make love in the fields to bring fertility to crops and offer themselves to men not only for their own pleasure, but also to initiate them into the higher realms of consciousness. Sex also featured prominently in the rituals of goddess *worship*. The Celtic Feast of Beltane (sexual rituals on May Day) and the Greek "Eleusian mysteries" (feasts in homage to the goddess Demeter which included orgies and ecstatic dance) were celebrations of spring, of the Goddess rebirthing Herself. Human sexual activity combined with spirit was believed to release the "nectar of the Goddess," the very highest form of energy. Although this spirit could grow in anyone who channeled it, goddess worshipers believed it originated in a woman's body. Because the female body offered the gateway into spirit and new life, it was considered a temple, with the womb and genitals as its altar.

It's no surprise that many shrines to goddesses referred to female anatomy. Many holy places were built over wet, watery springs or caves, made into womb-shaped circles of stones or formed into earthen mounds resembling breasts. Huge rocks shaped like women's genitals were also considered holy.

Because goddesses were portrayed as sexually free, yet initiated into the sacred sides of sex, many were called "sacred prostitutes." They did not sell their services or use sex entirely for their own pleasure but as a sacred tool for ensuring the continuity of life, abundant crops, the well-being of others.[2] Some of these very same goddesses who were called prostitutes also spent long celibate periods, in which they didn't need or want lovers. So, just as they were given the not-very-accurate label of prostitute, they were also called virgin, although this didn't necessarily mean they were innocent or untouched. It meant they were unmarried, had no children or didn't tie their fate to a single man. Thus, it was possible for them to be both "virgin" and "whore" at the same time, with neither term being a slur and without implying a split personality.

It was precisely this openly sexual, independent, female-honoring aspect

[2]Ibid., 138.

of goddess cultures that later made goddesses and goddess worshipers into easy targets. When patriarchal religions started gathering forces approximately between 2500 and 1500 B.C., female-honoring cultures started to be emphatically, viciously and consistently stamped out. What women held as sacred, the new order held as perverse. The once-revered wise woman became "a witch." The "sacred prostitute" became a "whore" and "praying with the body" either through sex, dance or some other means was considered sinful. Women fell from grace, from goddess-incarnate to seductress and destroyer of men's power and virtue. As we know from the Old Testament, women were held responsible for the eviction from Paradise because the serpent, that old goddess symbol of wisdom and life everlasting, now the embodiment of evil, told Eve to take a bite from the Tree of Knowledge.

Whereas goddess cultures were Earth based, the patriarchal religions that hoped to destroy them were based in Heaven. Whereas goddess religions revered the body, patriarchal religions saw the body, particularly the *female* body, as dangerous. They quickly sought to separate spirit from flesh, as a way to keep the former clean. Of course, the mere evidence of human existence proves that this notion of preserving spirit without including sex and the body never really worked.

Those who sought to wipe out goddess cultures included (but weren't limited to) bands of warrior Anglo-Saxon nomads from the north of Europe and Asia, also the Romans, Hebrews, sons of Islam, and especially the Christian church, also the Spaniards, English and Portuguese who traveled into South and North America. It isn't really known why matriarchal cultures were so vehemently attacked. Perhaps it was just a normal cycle in the balance of power. After all, women seemed to hold the power for forty to seventy thousand years. No doubt, as men became aware of their role in procreation, they thought it was time to get some of the credit. But they didn't want to *share* the credit. They wanted it all. They pillaged the temples and artwork and retold the myths. Yet they were really the same stories told over and over again, like a whisper down the lane, with the original details altered to serve different gods.

The transition from Mother Goddess into Father God wasn't quick or clean. It took hundreds and, in some places, more than a thousand years. Yet goddess worship survived in spite of church edicts, the Inquisition, accusations of heresy, public shame and death by torture. Goddess religions continued to be practiced among peasants who lived off the land, beyond the control of the church. When it was no longer safe to worship goddesses, they transferred "goddess power" to saints and the Virgin Mary. People continued to pray to a divine feminine power because it was compassionate and addressed that side of us which is physical, real, both fragile and strong.

Although many women in modern times haven't been aware of the role that goddesses played in our history, the brutal eradication of our instinctive power has nonetheless rocked our collective memories. Historians estimate that during the three-hundred-year period of witch burnings, torture and persecution (between A.D. 1500 and 1800), anywhere between one hundred thousand and *nine million* women were executed because they engaged in many of the same things we practice today.[3] (According to Starhawk, the true number isn't known. The bigger estimate takes into account women who weren't executed but died in prison.)

If we listen closely, we can almost hear their screams inside of us. If we are still enough we almost feel their pain and the pain of millions of other women through time whose stories went unwritten, songs remained unsung, dances never got danced because it was dangerous to do so. No wonder we have been afraid to reconnect with who we were because there's no proof that the same type of persecution won't happen again. Although we live in a time when we can reembrace a divine feminine force and no longer be literally burned at the stake for it, we can still burn metaphorically in unfriendly territory. But with our spiritual history tucked in our pockets, we're beginning to realize on a large scale who we are and where we might be headed.

As Jean Shinoda Bolen wrote in her wonderful book *Goddesses in Every Woman* (Harper & Row, 1985), we each possess various aspects of different goddesses, either simultaneously, at different times of our lives or even different parts of the day. The goddesses inform us, inspire us. They *are* us. Although many of us modern women have thought of ourselves as blazing trails and crafting ourselves into "new women," in fact some of those trails were blazed a long time ago. We're simply finding our way back to them. Our ancestral sisters have left a rich, mythological legacy. They represent our missing pieces. This is important because if we know what's missing, we'll know what we need to feel whole.

"When the balance changed, the dark side of the feminine was also suppressed. The Goddess had been a model of woman's nature in all its fullness. The irrational, the chaotic, and destructive, which had been acknowledged when the Goddess reigned supreme, were split off from divinity and became feared."

—ELINOR GADON,
The Once and Future Goddess

[3]Starhawk, *Dreaming the Dark* (Boston: Beacon, 1982), 187–88.

Goddesses

The following list of goddesses is a primer for those who aren't familiar with goddesses or whose knowledge of mythology is rusty. This is by no means a complete list or description of each goddess. There are countless books that do that much better. It's meant to be a quick reference. Notice the similarities among the goddesses. Each is a compendium of contrasts, just as we are. Each mirrors another, just as we do. No one is more or less important than another. There is room for all of them just as there is room for each of us.

GREEK/ROMAN GODDESSES

Aphrodite/Venus. Goddess of love and beauty. Conceived in a marriage of feminine, watery earth and masculine sky, born of the sea. Had many lovers; the most famous was Aries/Mars. Had half a dozen children, all by different lovers, none of them by her husband.

Worship of Aphrodite split into two different sects (indicative of the growing separation between sex and spirit). *Aphrodite Urania* represented the beauty of the female spirit. In this guise she also represented vigor, a well-being born of "awakened" sexuality, the alive body, with energy used for achieving health and wisdom. *Aphrodite Pandemos* represented the lower aspects of physical lust and became the "patron saint" of prostitutes. Aphrodite was surrounded by priestesses, called "Horae" (from which we get the word *whore*), graceful dancers famous for their "Dance of the Hours," in which they marked the passage of time. Temples of both sacred and secular prostitution were built in Aphrodite's honor.

Her symbols were birds, fruits, flowers and fragrances.

Artemis/Diana. Virgin goddess of the hunt, independent and fleet-footed, Artemis ran barefoot through the forest with her bow and arrow slung over her shoulder and tunic cut short to let her bare legs run free. She was feared by men because one look from her could kill.

Not just a huntress, she was a protector of animals. Not simply a virgin, the multi-breasted statue of Artemis at Ephesus shows she was also a symbol of fertility. Although not a mother, she was the goddess women prayed to in childbirth to nurse them through pain. She was considered a war goddess and believed to be the patron goddess of the Amazons (themselves not merely warriors but peace-loving priestesses). But she was also the Moon goddess, a symbol of mutable energies, softness, darkness, harmony. Celebrations in her honor included full-moon gatherings with ritual dance.

Artemis was also transformed into a saint, as Saint Ursula. (Her Anglo-Saxon name came from "Ursa" which means "bear.")

Her symbols include: the moon, the bow and arrow, the bear.

Demeter/Ceres. The Original Mother Earth, the goddess of agriculture. Mother of Persephone, who is the goddess of the Underworld. Demeter is a triple goddess, not only mother but symbolic daughter of Hecate, the moon goddess of death, who is the unspoken third point of the triad. Demeter's name literally translates as "de" the Greek symbol of three, the triangle, which also represents the triangle of the vulva and "meter" or mother.

Demeter stands at the center of the wheel of life—neither maiden nor crone and yet all of them at once, for she is mature, self-realized and represents that all aspects of the self can exist simultaneously, without conflict.

It was believed that Demeter made love in the fields of Eleusis to spread her fertility (thus the "Eleusian mysteries"). But when her daughter, Persephone, was abducted by Hades into the Underworld, Demeter was in such grief she made all the fields barren while she wandered the Earth searching for her. Eventually she struck up a deal with Zeus so that Persephone would return to the Earth for two-thirds of the year and spend the other third (a symbol of winter) in the Underworld.

Later Demeter was transformed into Saint Demetra and also Saint Demetrius, with many of her attributes (although not her sexual skills) transferred to them.

Her symbols include: corn stalks, seeds, jewels.

Hera/Juno. Most commonly known as the wife of Zeus—and a jealous wife at that. She is also the Greek goddess who most represents "hearth and home," or matrimonial domesticity, though her marriage was less than blissful.

During her young years, she was considered a "virgin" goddess only because she was unburdened by children or other responsibility. She was raped by Zeus, who appeared in disguise—and married him against her will. He had many indiscretions with mortals and other goddesses. She got revenge by ensnaring him and his lover in a net which she hung over the bed—and invited others to join in the mockery. Their disharmony was legendary and was believed to represent the very disharmony between the Goddess and God, the war between instinct and reason, female and male, moon and sun, dark and light. Hera was happier in her later years. She is a triple goddess whose myth traces her from youth, to mature married woman, to one who later lives more for herself.

Hera was also the reigning goddess of the "Heraea," competitive games that predated the Olympics. These games occurred in Argos and consisted of 160-yard footraces, run by bare-breasted women.[4] The competitors were broken into three age groups to honor the three phases of life. As in the Olympics, victors were rewarded with a wreath of olive branches.

Hera's main symbol is the hearth or "home fire."

Persephone/Proserpina. The original pure virgin maiden. Persephone was innocently picking flowers when she was abducted by Hades and taken to be his unwilling bride in the Underworld. There, Hades offered her a pomegranate to eat. Because she was hungry, she ate it. The bitter-tasting seed represented his sperm and the often bitter taste of sexual initiation, while its red and bulbous skin was a symbol of fruitfulness, fertility.

Persephone's descent into the Underworld is *the* symbol of initiation, both sexual and spiritual. Although she did not go to the Underworld by choice or willingly eat the pomegranate, she gained knowledge through experience and was changed forever. (When Eve bit the apple, she gained the same sort of knowledge. But Eve's legacy carried shame while Persephone's did not.) Persephone's journey rep-

---

[4]Patricia Managhan, *The Book of Goddesses and Heroines* (St. Paul, Minn.: Llewellyn, 1993), 153.

resents our own soul's plunge into darkness and subsequent awakening to wisdom.

Persephone's happy annual reunion with her mother was a symbol of the return to light but also a symbol of union within one being—the older woman possessing her maiden mind and the maiden possessing the knowledge and wisdom of her mother. This is a symbol of rescuing our own lost maidens and possessing ourselves as whole women. Persephone later grew into her more mature guise as Queen of the Underworld, where it was her job to comfort the souls of the dying and newly dead.

Persephone's most potent symbol is the pomegranate.

EGYPTIAN/MESOPOTAMIAN GODDESSES

Ishtar/Inanna. Babylonian goddess of love and giver of life but, like Aphrodite, had a complex nature and bad reputation. Perhaps the most infamous of the sacred prostitutes.

Ishtar's lover was her brother/son, Tammuz. When he died Ishtar descended (like Persephone) into the Underworld, dressed in her best attire. There she met the naked and "hairy goddess of death." To pass into the Underworld she had to dance through "seven-times-seven" gates and at each one had to divest herself of clothing and jewels, until at last she danced naked. This was the famous "Dance of the Seven Veils." While she danced, the Earth (as in the case of Demeter searching for Persephone) bore no fruits or crops. But through this dance, she won back the life of Tammuz, who, like Persephone, was able to live on the Earth for part of the year but had to return to the Underworld during winter.

Like Aphrodite, Ishtar had temples built in her honor and a following of "Horae" who were priestesses, sacred prostitutes, businesswomen and perhaps the original belly dancers who, like Ishtar, danced with veils and a "sacred" hip scarf.

In the Bible, Ishtar became Salome, no longer life-giver but destroyer—lewd, salacious murderer of a holy man. Salome's mother was married to Herod the King, but that marriage was declared invalid by John the Baptist. Salome was entreated by her mother to dance for King Herod, who was so pleased with her striptease that he offered Salome anything she desired. What she asked for, in deference to her mother, was the head of John the Baptist, which was delivered on a plate. Salome's black reputation still taints the belly dancer.

Ishtar's symbols are: the hip sash, veils, jewels, the serpent; also the moon, stars and bones.

Isis. So primordial, she is thought to have given birth to the sun, Isis was called "the oldest of the old." Like Ishtar, Isis's lover Osiris was her brother, a twin with whom she reportedly engaged in sexual embrace right in the womb. Osiris was killed by another brother and thus, Isis, like Ishtar, set out to find the body and to bring him back to life. She found his drowned corpse stuffed in a chest and began the process of mummification to bring him back to life. But the evil brother again intervened and this time chopped Osiris's body into pieces and scattered them across the countryside. Isis found all the pieces except his penis and so fashioned one from a shaft of gold, brought him back to life and got pregnant on "the golden phallus." She gave birth to Horus, who grew up to be the Sun God, the father of all Pharaohs, whose very life ensured the ongoing fertility of life in Egypt. Like Aphrodite, Demeter and Ishtar, Isis became the symbol for the power of sex and its constructive role in the renewal of vigor, the life force.

One of Isis's symbols is the feather. Upon entering the land of the dead, a person's heart was weighed against a feather. If the heart and the feather were in balance (the heart was not weighted down by emotions), the dead person would pass into the afterlife. Isis's other symbol was the snake, the Egyptian hieroglyph for goddess. This same symbol later represented Queen Cleopatra who seemed to possess the powers of Isis and was known as the "serpent of the Nile."

INDIAN/HINDU GODDESSES

Durga. The Hindu warrior goddess, also the goddess of orgiastic ritual, therefore a "virgin-whore." She was created by gods. Later, because she killed a buffalo demon who attempted to rape her, the gods accepted her as a warrior and she excelled at this. She became known as the destroyer of evil. Durga took the gods' power to achieve her own glory.

She is often shown with many arms (a symbol of her strength) and riding a lion (a symbol of spiritual power) or killing the buffalo. Like Aphrodite and Ishtar, she was the goddess of sexual rites, of the wisdom gained through focused sexual energy. She is often depicted stamping out the destructive aspect of sexuality. Those born as a result of unchanneled, unfocused sexual abandon are often shown under Durga's feet.

Her symbols are the lion and the buffalo.

Kali. The most extreme face of the destructive feminine force. She is shown with her eyes bulging and tongue sticking out, a necklace of skulls dripping blood, death growing in her womb. She danced an ecstatic, orgiastic dance of death, "the dance that never ends." Kali was the original Mommy Dearest, the extreme negative fantasy of the destructive mother, whose yoni (vagina) was devouring and insatiable.

But Kali is almost a cartoon, a mockery of herself. It is believed that once Kali is faced, she is not feared. Like many Hindu goddesses, Kali was a lover of the god Shiva, who was the "eternal dancer," the "dancer at the center of the universe," shown dancing in an all-consuming ring of fire as god of both creation and destruction. But Kali was the lover of his dark, destructive side. Like Aphrodite and Ishtar, Kali was attended by priestesses. Like Demeter and Hera, Kali was considered a triple goddess. Her priestesses were yoginis, or practitioners of yoga (of which Shiva was the inventor), shaktis ("shakti" was a generic name for mother as well as the name of a famous goddess) and dakinis or skywalkers (old women who, like Persephone, attended the souls of the dying).

Kali's symbols are: skulls, severed hands and blood.

Shakti. The favorite consort of Shiva. Through sexual union, Shakti supplied Shiva with "prana" and "apana," energy created from spirit and the body. These gave him the power to carry forth his task of tramping out ignorance and fear so that he could fulfill his purpose of renewing life. Shakti was the protective spirit who invigorated him. Without Shakti, Shiva had no power to dance the dance of humanity. Without Shakti, his male and female energies were out of balance.

Shakti's symbols are the symbols of the Earth Goddess: water, the Underworld, the snake.

Sri Laksmi. Sri Laksmi is one of the most beloved Hindu goddesses (especially by men) since she represents, like Hera, the prosperous wife; but Sri Laksmi was dutiful, while Hera was not. However, like Hera, she didn't start that way. Before marriage she had many lovers but after marrying Vishnu became subdued and came to represent the orderliness of society when a marriage is stable. Older depictions of Sri Laksmi show her emerging from a life-giving lotus, one hand on a full breast, the other pointing to her vulva. Modern depictions show her clothed but, like Ishtar, resplendent with jewels. She is often shown wearing a crown, bracelets, fine clothing and a red dot of beauty at the center of her forehead. She is the picture of well-being, the wealth of body and soul when all forces are in balance. She was an Earth goddess, a symbol of moisture and abundance, not in its primitive form, but in an aspect that is cultured, prosperous and royal.

Her image is one of moderation, respect. She is clearly the embodiment of vital energy, a sexual being. In fact, she and Vishnu are often represented as one bisexual person, merged into each other.

Like Aphrodite and Ishtar, Sri Lakshmi was honored by dancers—actual professional temple dancers called devadasis who also acted as "sacred prostitutes."

Sri Laksmi's main symbol is the lotus (a flower that blooms out of mud).

CHINESE/TIBETAN GODDESS

Kuan Yin/Tara. The Buddhist goddess of compassion, purity, wisdom and the most beloved Chinese female figure (called Tara in Tibetan tradition). Kuan Yin's name means "she who hears the weeping of the world," and she is perhaps the most prayed-to female holy figure on the planet. Instead of choosing enlightenment and a return to pure energy, Kuan Yin chose to stay human so she could perform acts of compassion. Like the Virgin Mary she was a virgin goddess without the shadow/whore side. Her womb produced the world, but not children. Like the dakinis and Persephone, she was believed to be the comforter of dying souls.

Kuan Yin's symbols include the magic peach and the pearl—offerings of compassion.

CELTIC GODDESS

Brigit. The Celtic protector of poets, goddess of healing, medicine and also ironwork (for which she carried a magic cauldron—a symbol of alchemical transformation. This alludes to the notion that Brigit could transform sex into wisdom the way alchemists reportedly turned base metal to gold). To the Druids, a Celtic, Earth-worshiping spiritual order of sorcerers, priestesses and priests, she represented inspiration and divination.

She was yet another "virgin-whore." Like Ishtar, Aphrodite and Kali, Brigit was attended by priestesses, who were known as sacred prostitutes. Although supposedly no men were allowed into the cult of Brigit, rites in her honor included times of abstinence followed by sexual feasting.

She was also a triple goddess and therefore was depicted with three faces: the "sister" virgin, the Nature goddess/mature lover and the dark mother of the Underworld. She has been considered the patroness for those who, like Persephone, take on an Underworld quest or spiritual journey.

Brigit was such a beloved goddess that she, too, like Demeter, was turned into a saint. Brigit's feast day (February 1), a pagan holiday representing Brigit's return from the Underworld (and thus the first open window to spring), later became known in the Catholic Church as "the purification of the Virgin," or Candlemas. It is still a pagan holiday observed by many.

Brigit's symbols include the snake, the cauldron, the forge and the magic well.

Mayan/Aztec Goddess

Coatlicue, The Lady of the Serpent Skirt. Aztec goddess of love and death, creation and destruction. The mother of all deities who took the dead into her body and rebirthed them. She is shown, like Kali, with a skull inside her womb, a necklace of skulls or severed hands around her neck. Her skirt of serpents also represents the penises of many lovers. It was also believed that every night she devoured the sun and every morning birthed it again.

She was both mother and lover of Quetzalcoatl, the beloved god of the Aztecs and Mayans, who created language, arts and the famous Mayan calendar. Upon return from the Underworld, Quetzalcoatl returned with a bag of bones. Coatlicue ground them up in a vessel to which he added his semen and thus a new race of people was born.

Quetzalcoatl is often shown in the jaws of the feathered serpent—either being devoured or rising up out of the Underworld. The feathered serpent from which he ascends or descends represents his union with the Earth Goddess, Coatlicue, his mother and lover, mistress of life, death and rebirth.

Coatlicue's symbols are the serpent and feathers.

Christian Goddess

The Virgin Mary/Black Madonna. The Virgin Mary is the divine feminine force of the Christian tradition. I've saved Her for last because She has had the most profound effect on women in our culture. Mary represents the separation of body and spirit and everything the Earth Goddess (and human female) was not (while her dark namesake, the repentant "whore" Mary Magdalene seemed to represent one who has successfully converted from a goddess religion to God). Yet the Goddess is woven into the Virgin Mary's history as well.

Like many of the goddesses, Mary drew some of her power from her ability to bear a child. Yet this posed a problem for the new patriarchy because they did not want the mother of their savior to have any associations with the earthy sensuality of the goddess traditions they were trying so hard to wipe out. So Mary's conception of Christ was explained not as a base human function but a celibate act of God, a visit from a spirit-offering angel with the details of conception vague.

This singular ascension to impossible purity has been at the root of serious conflicts that have persisted for women ever since. Mary represents not the successful *transformation* of sexual energy into pure spirit, as in Goddess (and later Tantric and Taoist) traditions, but a successful severance of it all together. It's a piety that draws none of its power from the body but thrives, in spite of it, as a victor over evil. For two thousand years, Mary has been the main female representative of the holy power of God. But real women have never been able to live up to her ideal. To be like Mary, we could never be sexual. To be sexual we could never be like Mary. To be a devout Christian still means totally accepting the literal notion of the virgin birth, rather than its metaphor. In our age of science and pragmatic realism, this belief can alienate many.

The Virgin Mary was problematic for the Church in other ways. In the twelfth century, Mary's popularity reached such a peak that hundreds of churches and cathedrals (such as Chartres and Notre Dame) were built in her honor, eclipsing the worship of Christ and God the Father. Many of these were even built on former shrines to goddesses. Common, pagan folk simply transferred their beliefs in various goddesses onto the Virgin Mary. They believed that Mary possessed Earth wisdom and the power to grant or withhold fertility. Thus Mary was often shown, like Demeter, holding shafts of wheat and corn. Mary and Demeter also gave birth to their children at the same time of year. Demeter had Persephone on the winter solstice, "the return of the light," while the birthday of Jesus falls three days later.

In the Middle Ages, the Church had another "Virgin Mary problem." Hundreds, if not thousands, of Black Madonnas started to appear throughout Europe and Latin America. The blackened hands and faces of the Virgin were often explained away as some kind of color degeneration—degeneration that oddly didn't affect anything but the skin on all those pieces of art. Black Madonnas were thought to possess "the manna of the old Goddess of life, death and rebirth . . . , an extra-physical power immanent in and emanating from nature, viewed as the embodiment of all elemental forces that produce and maintain the order of the universe."[5] These Black Madonnas were such a threat to the Church because it wasn't in keeping with Christian tradition for a woman to have such power.

Many of Mary's symbols first appeared as goddess symbols: wheat, corn, the moon, the sacred girdle or hip scarf (which Mary reportedly lost as she was carried up to Heaven. This relic was supposedly housed at Chartres Cathedral). Mary is often portrayed sitting on a jeweled throne, aglow in a radiant light.

Although the power that goddesses possessed seems beyond our reach, the myths remind us that our lives contain magic, too. For every one of our dark and shining moments, there is a goddess who represents that aspect of ourselves. Even when they highlight our least favorite behaviors, somehow the presence of a goddess and her myth brings us comfort and inspiration. They remind us that we, too, are changeable, that we can be all things and can switch between various states at will.

[5]Elinor Gadon, *The Once and Future Goddess* (San Francisco: Harper, 1989), 218.

3

Every One of Us Is a Goddess

Every one of us is born with a feel for our power. When we are babies, we discover how our cries bring food, mother, a warm embrace; we also learn that not every desire gets met. But we keep trying. With even the slightest encouragement, we can grow into fearless little girls, tromping out to conquer the neighborhood, play aggressive games, climb trees, beat up boys. Even in our more traditional "girl" worlds of dolls and dress up, we use make-believe to speak our hearts' desires. We know what we want, go after both worldly goods and affection and suffer no conflict about it. There's no such thing as a separation between the physical and spiritual.

Following Persephone

But when we hit puberty, our power fails us. We become clouded with hormones, full of conflict and confusing messages about how we should or shouldn't be now that our bodies are "mature." Our bodies suddenly seem to grow out of control. Once small, fast and hungry, they grow heavier, slower and softer with a new glaze of fat. The boys we once left in the dust now leave us behind, hit harder, throw farther, lift heavier. One season our power is in full force; the next it's gone and in its place come doubt, fear and the specter of sex. Our minds, once hungry for information, get cluttered up with a need for approval. We start to compare ourselves, our bodies, hair, confidence and popularity with cover girls, prom queens, one another and often put ourselves on the B list—the ugly, fat, untalented and, worst of all, unpopular—not like everyone else.

For many of us, puberty marks the transition from spotlight into shadow. As Mary Pipher pointed out in *Reviving Ophelia* (Ballantine, 1994), this is the age when girls' math scores typically drop, IQs plummet and boys zoom ahead, grabbing the attention of teachers at school.[1] Meanwhile, we fill ourselves with sweets and fats to fill the void and, without guidance, abandon sports, hobbies, more "aggressive" body-centered activities and drift instead toward lethargy.

We don't like falling from physical grace, so instead we often go numb. It takes a strong sense of self and internal drive just to keep moving. It takes determination, as well as supportive parents (with money to spend on lessons) to continue with sports, go to dance class or gymnastics, study the piano, drawing, act in a play or sing in a choir instead of following the herd to the burger joint. If we admire and emulate healthy, active women, then we stand a better chance of surviving adolescence with some sense of our power. If we find camaraderie in healthy group activities, we find friends and a way to define ourselves. But if we lack "role models" or feel that playing sports, dancing, singing or doing something else that excites us exacts too high a toll on a "normal teenage life," we'll give it up so we can fit into a group. If we still harbor a dream to be team captain, leading lady or class president but encounter resistance along the way, we'll be inclined to give up if we interpret resistance as failure. We may learn to stop trying or discover how to disappear. We may also cut ourselves off from the things we once loved to do so others won't judge us for it—and even take pride in our ability to do without, the way an anorexic feels superior for her ability to live without food.

This is the time when we buy into the separation between body and spirit. A war begins between how we're "supposed to be" and how we are. Our hormones flood us with desires while our parents, teachers, friends and the media flood us with rules on how to be. We learn that having sex, eating too much food and being fat are bad. Abstinence, being thin and dieting are good. Thus, we fall into "the hell cycle," fluctuating between denial and indulgence sometimes day by day or minute by minute.

[1]Mary Pipher, Ph.D., *Reviving Ophelia* (New York: Ballantine, 1994), 62.

In adolescence we enter the Underworld for the first time and the spell of sleepy forgetfulness is cast. We eat junk food and accept slobbery kisses because, like Persephone, we're hungry and don't know anything better. We travel a long way from our wild but directed, ravenous but disciplined, imaginative but raw, original selves.

We discover the power of sex and confuse it with our internal power. Sex or sex appeal may get us attention, "love" and worldly goods, but if we depend on it, we tend to draw our self-worth from how others treat us. We don't hold the flame ourselves. We think it all comes from outside. Yet, like Persephone, we find that we have to swallow the consequences of our actions.

Should we become addicted to drugs or alcohol, have a baby too young, devote ourselves to an abusive lover, join a gang, cult or worship a self-styled mystic, entertain thoughts of suicide, commit a crime and go to jail, or even just try to have a career, a marriage and a child all at once, while still in our late teens or early twenties, we place more obstacles between ourselves and the power that once grew in our core. We don't come into ourselves until much later, if at all. Many of us then stay in the Underworld out of habit. We don't even know that we've forgotten who we are or who we could be.

This first trip to the Underworld is a test, the first surrender of our power. If we pass out of it and find the strength of our own convictions, we earn more power through a deeper knowledge of the world and our place in it. We learn to value ourselves. But we can easily use this experience as an excuse to become victims and stay trapped in delusion. We may look back upon the magic power we once felt as girls as nothing more than childishness.

The best way to turn a trip to the Underworld into an initiation and not simply a life of hell is to stay sober in the process and maintain some form of physical activity. It's not easy, I know, especially for teens who think that physical activity is "uncool" or that drug and alcohol indulgence are normal rites of passage that they shouldn't be denied. But respect for the body is *the* safety line back to sanity and everyday life on Earth. This is true at any age.

Our lives are dotted with trips to the Underworld. As we get older, we can even find that it's a place of recovery, rest and rejuvenation, a place not to fear but embrace, especially if we go there sober and awake in our skin—and resist the temptation to float down the river of drug-induced sleep. Many of us even go there by choice to sit in silence and let a life cycle die so another can be reborn. But when we're younger it just feels like the death of dreams. What it is, however, is a test of faith and a time of fallow, so our fields can bring forth a greater harvest in the future.

Those of us who make it through the winter, burst forth into a new phase in our lives. Like bears emerging from hibernation, we leave the Underworld slightly weakened but also refreshed and ravenous and ready to take on new tasks. Each time we descend and emerge, we reclaim another piece of ourselves.

Demeter's Dance

"I believe the real task for women's transformation these days is to discover for themselves who they are. But parts of this discovery entail a dialogue with their history, with the developmental influences that have affected them personally, culturally and spiritually."

—LINDA SCHIERSE LEONARD, *The Wounded Woman*

In our thirties and forties, we emerge from the fog of youth and enter our busy building years, still somewhat distracted from the core of who we are because our attention is on work, children, families. But we start to become aware that the various pieces of our lives now add up to something, although, perhaps, not quite what we expected. Our jobs (careers or day labor), houses (rented or owned), children (yes or no), net worth (or lack thereof), have landed us on specialized mailing lists and we're grouped accordingly, based on what we've done, what we earn and what we own—not so much on who we are. Even if we've leaped from job to job, city to city and relationship to relationship, in the hopes of avoiding such labels, we don't escape them.

Thus, we begin Demeter's dance. Although not a "dancer," per se, not in the lusty and veiled tradition of Ishtar, Demeter dances (like Shiva) in the center of the wheel of life. Hers is the central point in the three-part story of maiden-mother-crone, of past-present-future, spirit-body-mind. She dances the fury of a woman who realizes that what was lost must be replaced or her fields will grow nothing—this season or all to come. Hers is a search for the missing pieces that she *must* weave into a new creation or will never feel complete.

Like Demeter, we don't necessarily volunteer to do this dance. It simply presents itself and so it must be danced, regardless. Demeter's dance takes courage, for it means another trip to the Underworld to rescue the lost girl; but it is a spiraling return, another rotation with the same shape as the original yet with a wiser and more informed perspective. It is our dance in the middle third of life, looking back to what we surrendered and forward to whom we shall be, with or without this piece. It comes just when we don't have time for it, when we're perched between two generations, occasionally taking care of them both, with little time for ourselves. As it begins, we start to realize, with the subtlety of a sledgehammer, that no one else is responsible for our lives—not our parents, children, siblings, spouses, bosses, friends or communities we live in. However we yearn to create our world, we'd better get on with it. Whomever we hope to become, we'd better make a plan. All the busy-ness we may have erected around who we think we are starts to crumble. The lost girl finally begins to emerge. If we ignore her or run the other way, hoping to stay in our clean, linear, adult lives, we subconsciously create other ways to bring her out: we get fired from our jobs, get sick or depressed, have accidents, get divorced. These challenges present us with more time to think and feel. Our dream lives become more vivid. A new face begins to emerge in the mirror. We begin to embrace the truth of who we are, remember who we once wanted to be, and get to decide who we may become. But it's no longer theoretical. These things are based on actions and attitudes. So we must bravely take up the sword and with a clean cut, chop away what no longer works in our lives. This creates a clearing—like throwing out old clothes, so we can take stock of what we own and prepare for the new. Once we do this, we pass through the pain and begin to own ourselves at last. Often we realize that what may have first looked like a terrible passage was, in fact, a gift.

This can be a rough passage for those of us who lack stubborn determination, unfounded optimism or even a healthy dose of denial to see us through. According to the U.S. World Health Organization, the U.S. suicide rate for women is second highest during this time in our lives, between ages thirty-five and fifty-four. The highest rates occur between fifty-five and sixty-four—which clearly tells us that if we're depressed in the middle stage of life and fail to take action to satisfy our soul's longing, the black devil depression may get us later. The spark of girl power that we rescue in our middle years can provide a foundation for the rest of our lives.

It takes courage to look at the dreams we abandoned and why. It takes stubbornness to ignore others' objections when our changes don't serve them. It takes a bit of inspired insanity to figure out how to have this original piece of ourselves and make it work in our grown-up lives. The only way to do Demeter's dance is roll with it, dump what no longer serves, cleanse our souls of negativity and be brave enough to declare, at least to ourselves, "This is what I need," then go after it and enjoy.

"If a woman is caught in an over-extended lifestyle or achievement-oriented values, depression or illness may offer the only opportunity to allow her to be with herself."

—JUDITH DUERK,
*Circle of Stones,
Woman's Journey to
Herself*

"Ours is a search for meaning, for that which has been lost and for what can be."

—ELINOR GADON,
*The Once and Future
Goddess*

Few of us make it to the center of the wheel of life without black marks all over our hearts and histories. What Demeter's dance offers us is a graceful way to alter our relationship with pain and reclaim our magic. It is pain that gives us our stories after all, our badges of survival, compassion, determination, sense of humor and most important, our ability to transcend. But it is our magic that transports us back into the power we first felt as girls and the power that awaits.

The Triple Goddess and the Alchemy of Age

With this treasure in our pockets, we grow into our fullness. We enter not only the second, mother, stage more complete but also the third, wise-crone, stage of a triple goddess. It's an age of unification and contradiction. Both the dark and light sides become more extreme. We're tougher, yet more sensitive. We're more opinionated but we know the power of silence. As we clock more time, the differences between the three faces of the goddess become *less* pronounced, not more so. In one minute we can laugh like a maiden, nurture or nag like a mother, and hobble like a crone. It isn't necessarily age that gives us this ability. It's the depth of our souls. We don't have to be fifteen to feel like maidens or fifty-five, and older, to feel wise. We just need to use our senses.

In her groundbreaking book *A Woman's Book of Life: The Biology, Psychology and Spirituality of the Feminine Life Cycle* (Riverhead, 1997), and in her lectures, Joan Borysenko refers to a formerly unmarked *fourth* cycle in the usual three-part triptych of a goddess-woman's life. Because our life spans have almost doubled in the last hundred and fifty years, Ms. Borysenko claims it's time to update the old three-part model. Our maiden years have gotten shorter, our mid-life years have gotten longer and our crone years have become less "crone-like" as the world fills with beautiful, vibrant "old ladies." But Ms. Borysenko also identifies an entirely new cycle, which up until now hasn't been acknowledged. She believes this additional stage begins at age forty-nine, or the seventh cycle of seven years. She calls these our "jubilee years," when we are no longer maiden or mother and not yet crone. Women at this age, she says, possess wisdom, vigor, beauty, sensuality and "fierce power" that grows as estrogen levels drop and testosterone levels increase.

Typically, in past generations, women would enter their jubilee years just when, in the eyes of the culture, husbands and the advertising world, they became "invisible" and "asexual" and were often traded in for younger models. It seemed as if their jewels and furs were put into protective vaults but the women and their wisdom were thrown away. The beauty and sensuality of older women, not just in these precrone years but well beyond, has been touched upon only rarely in storytelling. The subject seems practically taboo. But that is changing as more of us age together and stubbornly, deliciously declare that, under the right circumstances, we are sexual creatures indeed!

The baby boom generation, of which I am a part, has the opportunity to literally change both the face and body of aging. Many of us are already devoted to the benefits of exercise. Movement can help us embark on a new kind of alchemy—the alchemy of aging. Our bodies have sense memories, after all. If we cultivate the awareness of what it feels like to be energetic, graceful and strong when we are younger, we can more easily access this sensation as we get older. We can even do this with no exercise history to draw from if, before we embark on a dance or exercise program, we "imagine" ourselves sensual and strong—literally enter the body of the woman we yearn to be even before we've built the body. Too often we do it the other way around. We expect that our sensuality and beauty will show up *after* we've re-created our bodies. But this is backwards—and it makes us wait too long. If we're sensual and beautiful now, the body *will* show up because we'll be more likely to follow through with actions that support our beliefs. If we already feel like a queen and not a toad, we'll be more likely to get up and move. It's easier on our bodies and psyches if we start this practice at a younger age. But it also doesn't matter all that much. Women over thirty tend to have rich, sensual inner lives. We can use this to inform our movements. Almost every one of us also played dress-up and make-believe as children. As odd as this may sound, we can use just this skill to create a new fantasy, a transformed self. It's not that much different from the games we played as girls, except our dress-up and subjects of make-believe are much more fun and exotic.

When we take this magic and blend it with movement, we enter an expanded sense of being. We become ultrapresent. This is our ticket into an ageless, "timeless zone." I feel this at work in my life. If I don't dance or do some other sort of workout for several days, my posture slumps, my mind gets fuzzy, my attitude goes sour, my metabolism slows down. I stumble out of bed in the morning, moan and start to believe that I'm "getting old."

"True immortality can be experienced here and now, in this living body. It comes when you draw the infusion of Being into everything you do."

—DEEPAK CHOPRA,
*Ageless Body,
Timeless Mind*

However, when I put on my leotard and walk into the dance studio, I am no longer a middle-aged woman with tight shoulders and creaky knees but a dancer of no discernible age, at least from a distance. Or when I imagine myself climbing hills like Artemis or lifting weights like a yogi, I also enter the "timeless zone." Such activity lets me call upon the light step of the maiden, the rooted and wide-hipped stance of the mother and the wisdom and deep soul of the wise old woman—all at once. When I stop moving, my age eventually creeps back, especially first thing in the morning. But during that period of timelessness, I could be any age, living in any century. I bend the rules of gravity and time.

There is a story about Marilyn Monroe walking down the street in New York with Truman Capote. Truman mentioned that no one was noticing her and wondered why. She said, "It's because I'm not being *her*." Without changing clothes or makeup, she then instantly switched into "Marilyn" the movie star and people recognized her immediately. I believe it's as simple as this. Each of us has a timeless dancer, a goddess, even a Marilyn inside who symbolizes our magic—and our ability to trick time, others and even ourselves. We just need to believe in her, do the things that delight her, turn on the switch and let her out.

4 Dancing Our Spirits

"Thousands of years ago, on the hilltops of central Anatolia and the Mediterranean, women enacted dance rites in honor of this Goddess (the Great Mother), rites from which men were excluded, as they were from all women's ceremonies concerned with fertility."

—WENDY BUONAVENTURA, *The Serpent of the Nile*

Dance is to women what sport and war are to men. It's our original language, primal and instinctive. Before we had words, we had hips to speak our stories. Most women understand at a cellular level how to communicate with our bodies, even if we lack the technical skill to do so. We watch dancers and recognize the blend of motion and emotion because those things are part of *us*. Dance leaps over logic and diminishes the boundaries between flesh and spirit, space and time. Dance is the art form that we wear *inside* our skin—and women, after all, are masters of the internal realm.

Our Dancing Roots

Many of us are "secret" dancers. Some of us dance alone in our rooms or let loose on a dance floor only after a couple of drinks. Some of us wander from class to class, teacher to teacher, searching for a "dancing high" and perhaps even a chance to perform. Yet, whether we have years of training or none at all, whether we have performed for adoring audiences or just the pictures on our walls, we mostly all crave the same things: to become conduits of grace, to be beautiful and strong, to paint our feelings on the air so that others can read them, to dwell in that magical place of the dance. And what is that place? It is, as it says in the myth of Shiva "the place of the human heart." It is not only *our* hearts that we feel beating but also the hearts of others who have pulled meaning from dance.

During the time of goddess cultures, when dance was used as an ecstatic, ritual, embodied prayer, we didn't study dance to the extent we do today. We just danced. Although not much information survives on how we did this, what we suppose from dancers caught on vase paintings, in statuary and on fresco walls is that we danced in the company of one another. We danced the flow of water, the flight of birds, the slither of snakes, the stories of our lives, the cycles of birth, death and rebirth. We danced the power of the Divine Feminine in a tribal circle of shared celebration. Our moves were soft, rounded, beautiful, mesmerizing, spontaneous and full of meaning. Our waving hips and torsos highlighted the very earthiness of our flesh. We did not use dance to become "lighter than air" as many dancers do today. We used it to fully inhabit our body-spirits and touch the Earth. Dance was also a group experience. It was not meant to be observed as much as danced. All participants, regardless of skill, size or age were "dancers."

When the patriarchal religions sought to wipe out everything pertaining to the Divine Feminine, the sacred dancer fell from grace and dance itself entered a long, dark time. Women who continued to do soft, sensual dances in honor of a feminine deity did so either in secret gatherings (mostly of other women), at their own peril, or they danced in remote places, on distant islands or deep in the countryside, far from the eyes of missionaries or the Church. When the body and spirit were regarded as one, such dancing represented the human spirit in its most exalted state. But when the body was declared separate from spirit—and women's bodies in particular were considered evil, any dance that seemed suggestive was considered "pagan" and immoral. The sacred dancer thus metamorphosed from "high priestess" into a woman of dubious moral character, one of the "horae," a "slut." Stripped of her holy roots, she no longer emulated the sacred tradition of Ishtar but the profane spirit of Salome.

Sensual, female dancing endured, however, because people never lost their fascination with dancing, dancers or sex. The "dancing girl" became an enduring figure on the landscape of dance history, whether she danced clothed or naked. All across the world, feasts, weddings and celebrations were not complete until the dancing girl appeared. She was not admired so much because her movements were full of sacred meaning or even because of her dancing skill. She was admired because she could be an object of others' desires.

In the last century, the dancing girl gained wide-scale popularity. Although, in most cases, she was no longer considered a "hora," she was still somewhat tainted by the past because dancing freely and sensually in public (especially when she danced alone) was thought of as odd if not indecent. This is still true today. The dancing girl has never earned a great deal of respect or money. She's often been used merely as set dressing. People have even assumed she was "available" for other services because she was so comfortable moving her body.

The dancing girl has had many changes of costume and played many parts. She's been the temple dancer, harem dancer, hootchie-kootchie dancer, taxi dancer, cancan girl, gypsy girl with the tambourine and hula girl. She's been given a platinum wig, tap shoes and miniskirt and cloned into the Ziegfeld Girl, a Busby Berkeley Beauty and a Radio City Music Hall Rockette. From time to time, she's been plucked from the chorus line and twirled around Hollywood movie sets by Fred Astaire or Gene Kelly. Or she's been launched into the stratosphere of immortality like Josephine Baker, Little Egypt, Sally Rand, Isadora Duncan, Ruth St. Denis, the writer Colette and many others whose dances blended sensuality and art.

The dancing girl is still alive and kicking. She's a go-go girl swinging in a cage above a disco. She's hoofing on Broadway. She's riding an elephant in the circus or hanging by her teeth from ropes. She's the showgirl in Vegas or on a cruise ship, decked out in feathers, G-string and heels. She's the wanna-be in auditions for those jobs where the first thing they say is "Okay, girls, let's see your boobies." She's even the high school cheerleader, or the grown-up Laker girl or the Dallas Cowgirl earning $25 to $50 a game (while the players take home $25,000 to $60,000). She may even be your aerobics teacher, making the rounds to Ms. Fitness, aerobics and body-building competitions hoping to take home a title, a trophy and endorsements. She works hard and does it for fun, exercise, for a hobby or to fulfill an artistic dream. In the extreme, she's the stripper or "exotic dancer"—just about the only one who can actually peddle her dance skills (if she has any) into a decent wage.

Obviously not all female dancers carry associations with "the dancing girl." Prima ballerinas, ballroom, modern, jazz and many ethnic dancers who represent high culture have successfully transcended the stigma. Ballet was the first dance style especially intended to contrast with the "vulgar street dances" of common people. It was fashioned to epitomize the refinement, culture and class of eighteenth-century French courtly life. It was performed only for royalty and the wealthiest members of society. Originally, however, ballet started in the fifteenth century as a highly symbolic dance style, based on the "alphabet of the Druids!"[1] The earliest ballet dancers were put on stage in particular formations: circles, squares and triangles. Circles represented "truth known." The square in the circle represented "virtuous design" and two triangles in a circle represented "supreme power."[2] But ballet makers in the eighteenth century abandoned all that. If they even knew about the Druidic connection at all, they did not look to Earth-worshiping pagans for inspiration! Instead they found all the story lines they needed in Greek theater. Although the ancient Greeks were pagans, too, and their epics contained pathos and passion, they also dealt with grand themes, beyond the messy concerns of daily human existence. The idea in ballet wasn't to celebrate Nature (or the body) but elegantly avoid it.

Even now, much of modern ballet seems to be less about reveling in the body than transcending it. Although the body is the ballet dancer's tool and modern ballets have since become more openly influenced by sensual and street dancing, the ballet dancer still projects an ethereal quality, as if the main challenge in life is to overcome gravity, muscle and bone. In ballet, the hips almost never sway and the center of balance doesn't seem to be housed in the pelvis (as it is for the rest of us) but up in the chest. Ballet dances always seem to portray the desire to go up, up, up into Heaven instead of down, down, down to touch the Earth.

Although ballet supplies the best foundation of grace and line for any aspiring dancer, gymnast, skater, diver or other "performing" athlete, it still carries some medieval influences: dancing on steel-pointed shoes, the unspoken but well understood body requirements, dress codes, the hair in a tight bun (which causes receding hairlines in girls as young as twelve). These things are enough to thoroughly stamp out the joy of movement in all but the most dedicated and disciplined would-be dancers. What makes it all worthwhile to those who stick with ballet is that moment when the muscles are warm, the movements effortless, the emotions pour out and the music, passion and motion all combine to create magic. The rules of gravity bend or are broken. This is the dancer's perfect moment.

[1] Joan Lawson, *A History of Ballet and Its Makers* (London: Sir Isaac Pitman & Sons, 1964), 17.
[2] Ibid., 19.

Unfortunately there have probably been more "ballet casualties" than success stories. Every day, in fact, I seem to hear another one. Many of us, it seems, have our own dark histories of dance to overcome. We got smacked with riding crops if we didn't point our toes or stand up straight. We were told to go on a diet at age *ten* to slim down before a dance recital. Or we were lined up in two lines—the hopefuls and the hopeless. The "hopefuls" were encouraged to pursue the mostly arduous life of "being a ballet dancer," while the "hopeless" gave up dance for good, convinced we were too fat, too tall, too hippy, too athletic, too hungry or too wild to have anything to do with ballet. Although many of us have since found satisfaction in other types of dance, fitness or sports, even now that old dance school terror can raise its head. We feel it all over again when we find ourselves in a new class with a teacher who demands we do something we can't or doesn't inspire us to learn. So we drift to the back row hoping to become invisible and bolt out the door the second the teacher turns away. As we get older, these moments become opportunities to use our power and listen to our bodies' wisdom when it says "Don't do this one" or "Try it another way—" and if the teacher gets upset, that's the teacher's problem. Or these become hints that what we really ought to do is "find our own dance."

It seems that many of us are doing just that, putting aside our fears and dancing again or for the first time ever. People have been flocking to all sorts of dance classes: samba, tango, flamenco, East and West Coast Swing, Middle Eastern dance, African dance, Indian temple dance, Native American dance, Irish dance, Scottish Highland dance, Hawaiian and Tahitian dance, ecstatic "trance dance," also ballet, jazz, modern and other types of ballroom dance in numbers as never before. The new students are all ages, but there are more and more beginners in their forties and fifties than ever before. It seems that we don't just want to be "secret dancers" anymore. We want to get out and do it.

We're returning to our dancing roots because so many of us have gotten bored parking ourselves on stationary bikes and timing ourselves like boiled eggs. We've grown weary of striving in vain for bodies that we'll never have and yearn to enjoy the bodies we do have. We want another sort of substance—time to come back into our bodies after having been in our heads all day. Perhaps we just want to air our demons, meet new people and burn a few calories in the process. Perhaps we want to celebrate our history or participate in a culture that intrigues us and adopt it as our own.

"Dance embodies the full range of emotions; thus it can reveal the Subtle Body of Tantra in all its glory."

—Nik Douglas and Penny Slinger, *Sexual Secrets*

Or perhaps we yearn to blend all these culturally diverse influences into a creation that reflects our own diversity. There is indeed a movement under way toward marrying rhythms and dances in a way that shows we all come from one world.

Although some of our flashiest dance skills fade with age, the joys we pull from dance actually increase over time. The passions that move the dance also become much stronger. Dancing can refresh a weary soul, keep our muscles loose, our bones strong, our joints mobile, our hormones in balance, our minds at ease and our youth closer at hand. If we can dance today, we can probably dance tomorrow, perhaps even better, as long as we choose a dance that "fits" and know when not to push too hard. When we keep dancing, we keep our dancing spirits alive and always well within our reach.

The Straight and Bottom Line

So where do we go for the earthy, sensuous, hip-swaying motions that could help us celebrate our *womanly* spirit-bodies? We can go to Middle Eastern dance classes, Polynesian or hula classes, some modern dance classes, African, Haitian, Cuban, salsa or samba. We can find these classes in dance schools, recreational centers and community colleges. Or we can use the dance formula presented in this book to create dances of our own. Health clubs, gyms and aerobic studios for the most part still shy away from offering dance. The "D" word threatens people who view dance as "too girlie," too difficult to follow and not a real workout.

In the 1980s, the fitness industry neutered the term *aerobic dance* in order to entice men to join the classes. But after more than a decade, still only a tiny percentage of class participants are men—yet the dominant movement style in aerobics is still hard, quick and militaristic. Women dominate these classes, not because we love them but because we think we need them and they're usually the only game in town. We haven't yet reclaimed our natural, feminine moving style and incorporated it into our exercise routines. Perhaps we're afraid it doesn't "work." Perhaps we doubt our power.

What we typically find in most fitness classes are moves that go up, up, down, down or side to side, with arms and legs often squiggling out from an unsupported center like a dying bug. These are modern *war* dances, logic in physical form, a ceremony in honor of things man-made. They are more about battling our bodies than luxuriating in them. Their dominant spirit is "push-push." Thus we rush from our "push-push" lives into more of the same with no sanctuary for our feminine souls, rounded, three-dimensional bodies or the still point within. If not here, when or where do we get to "dance the Divine Feminine"? The workout slot is the perfect opportunity and is, therefore, ripe for a makeover.

Many of us in the modern world have to relearn how to move our hips! When we try, we often move our whole bodies—legs, back and shoulders because the hips are "frozen." This is so common in our country, particularly among men, that it borders on epidemic. Although such motions come naturally to women, we shy away from them because they emphasize the area of our bodies we most dislike. Plus, in many people's minds, any hip, butt or tail wagging still looks too suggestive. Despite our seemingly open attitudes about sex, this shouldn't seem to present a problem. It does, though, because the sexuality this sort of movement inspires is authentic, felt. It is not about mimicking sex, the way "exotic" dancers do. It is about connecting with the area in our bodies where we experience our sexuality and our power.

The nineties trend in fitness, particularly in videos, has been to address body parts chunk by chunk (one day legs, next day upper body, etc.). Yes, when it comes to strengthening body parts, especially with weights, it makes sense to isolate one muscle group at a time and hold everything else still. The next logical evolutionary step is to put all these disconnected parts back together again into an informed whole, find the center and connect with it—not with a hundred stomach crunches but with full-body motion that springs from the core.

To connect with the center doesn't take years of training. It takes sensitivity and being still enough just to feel. It helps when the conditions are favorable, when the moves are soft and inspire a going-within and when the music doesn't assault the senses but bears the loving hand of human touch. It's easier, too, when the clothes we wear celebrate our charms and move as we move, rather than highlighting our faults or hiding our flaws under a sexless bag.

The straight-and-bottom-line approach to fitness has been the dominant mode for the last twenty years, and it still serves a purpose. We need the straight line in sports, weight lifting and even in dance to make a point. We need the bottom-line results to make sure we aren't wasting our time.

These things kick us out of inertia and prepare us to fight other battles in our lives. Because of them, millions of us have reaped physical benefits, know how to give ourselves "physical therapy" when we're feeling low and possess tangible proof that exercise works. But this approach only represents half of who we are. The other side, collectively among us, is rumbling to be reborn.

PART TWO

Body and Shapes

5   The Seat of Our Power

"Instead of saying 'I hate my hips' we might say 'I keep dumping all my hate into my hips and growing them bigger to hold it all.'"

—BARBARA BRENNAN, *Light Emerging*

Ancient statues of fertility goddesses like the famously ample Venus of Willendorf and the stone statues on the island of Malta celebrated and revered women who, in our society, would be considered obese. These ancient goddesses seemed, like the universe, to possess the ability to expand indefinitely. Now, the notion of expanding indefinitely, especially in our hips, seems like a cruel and horrible fate. Back then, being large was probably the best insurance against starvation. But now, it's a sign of being "out of control." Women's hips are no longer a symbol of the mysteries and cycles of life; we have scientific explanations for all that. Wide hips have become, instead, a dumping ground for what we think is wrong with our bodies and ourselves. But in fact, our hip phobia highlights not so much what's wrong with us but with our culture.

The Pelvis

The pelvis is our power source. It's wide, expressive, creative, and oh so sensual. It's our root (the one that "grounds" us to the Earth), our rock (it gives us indisputable presence), our cradle (for carrying babies into flesh), our magic well (where our life energy originates), a mini cage for our organs and the great command central through which all full-body motions must pass.

The word *pelvis* means "basin," implying a cavity, depression, a watershed—an open, welcoming sort of architecture. The term *pelvic girdle*, however, implies contradiction, puts a lasso on the moon. To "girdle" a tree, in fact, means to tie a tight band around the trunk in order to kill it. These terms reflect the confusion and discomfort we hold about this area. The pelvis simultaneously holds a treasure to be sought and extra baggage to be destroyed.

Many women in recent decades have sought to be thin hipped and broad shouldered and have worked hard for a body type that is essentially mini male (except for the breast, of course, where larger is supposed to be better). Many of us believe this combo of slim hips and big breasts will help us get further ahead in the male world. It certainly helps Hollywood starlets. Narrow hips also let us run faster. Broad shoulders help us haul our own weight and shoulder burdens—important attributes for the woman who yearns to keep pace. Large breasts, of course, bring immediate attention and are there for default when other abilities fail.

But we've lost our capacity to see beauty in the most common female body type: broad pelvis, fleshy thighs, soft, rounded belly, narrow shoulders and "average"-sized breasts—a body type that has been celebrated in luscious paintings and sculptures for centuries but isn't celebrated now. Few modern women in America (and elsewhere where Western influence is felt) take pleasure in "owning our hips." It isn't part of our plan to really *feel* what's there, take up large amounts of space or really *dance* with these hips of ours. We plan to celebrate *after* the weight is off as a reward for denial and suffering. Perhaps if we celebrated ourselves *first*—hips, butt, belly and all—the excess would more happily slide off since it wouldn't be surrounded by so much negativity.

Our pelvic girdles and all they contain are also deeply tied to our sexual histories—both the erotic and the traumatic. They hold the threat or promise of pregnancy, the mess and pain of menstruation and elimination. The pelvis, therefore, is not perhaps the most enticing part of our bodies in which to take a physical, emotional and psychological "fantastic journey" because we don't know what we'll find there. Yet, I don't believe it's necessary to root out every emotion stored in our hips, do primal therapy or even hard labor on exercise equipment to make peace with the pelvis. I believe the best medicine is to highlight our hips with rocking, pelvic motions, even adorn them in beautiful scarves and take them out to play!

I guarantee that if there were more places where women of all ages,

"Pelvic movement and undulation was not a matter of sensation or pleasure but of life and unity with the active."

—Julie Russo Miskin and Marta Schill, *The Complete Belly Dancer*

"Energy should be circulated through the body so that no part of it is starved of vitality . . . The secret is to keep the body moving continuously and harmoniously, as through dancing. Movement can be very subtle and should be linked to conscious visualization of the energy flow."

—Nik Douglas and Penny Slinger, *The Alchemy of Ecstasy*

sizes and levels of ability could tie beads, tassels and chiffon around our hips, shake, shimmy, swivel and grind without fear of judgment and liberate our spirits in the process, we'd storm the doors to this experience. The problem of "exercise adherence" would go away. We'd have another problem of not wanting to do anything but dance!

But this isn't what happens. Very few of us exercise to celebrate ourselves—especially our hips. Most of us work out to lose weight. This is backward. Losing weight should be a *fringe benefit,* not the main, driving force behind working out. Exercise in this spirit is struggle instead of fun, and who wants to stick with that? Those of us who want to lose weight would be better off finding an activity we enjoy enough to *do* on a regular basis—even if it doesn't qualify as a " vigorous workout" and doesn't even promote "weight loss." When we love it, we do it and when we do it more days than not, the weight sometimes comes off by itself. And if it doesn't, at least the activity keeps us healthy.

Steven Blair, an epidemiologist at the Cooper Institute for Aerobic Research in Dallas, Texas, discovered in a recent study that people with even twenty-five to seventy-five "extra" pounds were healthy as long as they took some regular exercise. In contrast, he discovered that thin people who *didn't* take regular workouts had no extra protection against illness or early death.[1] Blair's study was a direct contradiction to earlier alarming headlines (based on a surgeon general's report and a Harvard study by JoAnn Manson and Walter Willet) which told us that being even *twenty* pounds overweight makes us prone to disease and early death.[2] Since many Americans are at least twenty pounds overweight, this made many people wrong from the start. The natural human response to such dismal news is "Well, if I'm already failing the test, why continue? Pass the cookies." Blair's study may have come as a jolt to inactive thin people, but it offered relief to larger people. His findings seemed to say "You can be fat and be fit. So go out and move." I also say you can be large and graceful. Go out and dance.

The sort of dancing I describe in chapter 7 is suitable for large-, average- and small-sized women—because it's not our size that determines our level of grace or ability. It also works equally well for the "unfit" as it does for the already fit, since these motions encourage us to *ease* our way into fitness yet also create a high degree of muscular control. Many of the movements

[1] Laura Fraser, *Health Magazine* (May/June 1996), 78.
[2] Ibid., 79.

also originate in the *pelvis*. So let's take a closer look at the pelvis and everything that goes on here:

• All big movements must, at some point, pass through the pelvis. The pelvis marks the body's center of gravity. It's here our balance resides. The "stabilizing" muscles that surround the pelvis keep us from falling over. The more we use our pelvis as the *source* of motion, the more we strengthen these stabilizers.

• A woman's pelvis is wider than a man's, the bones smaller but broader, the opening wider for giving birth. We have better mobility in our hips, so we can snake, shimmy and hip bump with greater ease (a great plus!). Since we have less upper-body strength than men, we rely more on leg power. Leg work can increase the stability of the pelvis—but only if the stabilizing muscles are somewhat strong to begin with. Otherwise we fall over or divert the load to other muscles—like the lower back.

• The pelvis is sturdy, the design more rugged than the shoulders, which have a similar ball-and-socket design. The hip joints are deep, the head of the bone more spherical, less likely to dislocate or get injured. Thus, hips are capable of big expressive movements, with less risk of injury. Also, the muscles that originate in this area are large and, therefore, eat up energy—i.e., burn calories.

• Our center of gravity sits at the top of the pelvis—about two to three inches below the navel—and about 1 to 2 percent lower in proportion than a man's (we are "lower riders"). In babies, this center of gravity starts just *above* the navel, then begins its descent. At age five, it drops to just below the navel, at age thirteen it's one inch below, at age seventeen it's anywhere from one to two inches below and finally in adulthood it drops to two to three inches below.[3] In essence, we descend into our rootedness as we age and settle over time into our hips. Thus, with age we become even more well suited to moving from our pelvic centers.

• Many of our organs are housed in and around the pelvis: the small and large intestine, the colon, ovaries and uterus, genitals and anus. We also wear three layers of trunk muscles in front, as a fibrous, multidirectional

[3]Marlene J. Adrian and John M. Cooper, *Biomechanics of Human Movement* (Madison, Wis.: Wm. C. Brown Communications, 1995), 31.

organic girdle, to hold everything in place: rectus abdominus, transverse (the hammock-shaped one that gets most stretched during pregnancy) and obliques. Movements that originate in the pelvis work these muscles from many angles and provide an internal massage for organs.

• The pelvis is a busy intersection of even more muscular activity. The pelvis sports the largest muscles in the body—the gluteus and its cohorts (the minimus, medius et al.). Hamstrings, quads, iliopsoas, inner and outer thigh all pass through the pelvis, connecting legs to torso. Other muscles that cross the hip joint allow legs to flex, extend, rotate in and out, abduct (open away from the midline of the body) or adduct (cross it). All have the power to enhance proper alignment or destroy it.

• In pregnancy the hips (and all other joints) expand for birth. The hormone relaxin loosens up the connective tissue and joints stay loose for up to a year after birth (this is believed to last as long as a woman nurses). Eventually the joints spring back to normal as the hormone subsides. But "the birthing year" leaves women more vulnerable to injury, especially in the pelvis. Women who are very flexible are at highest risk when taking stretches, especially *hip* stretches too far during this time. Sensitive connective tissue takes longer than muscle to heal.

When the Bow Breaks . . .

As we age we tend to use our bodies less and our hips almost not at all, focusing instead on the heart, mind and soul—in preparation, I suppose, for the journey *out* of our bodies—well before we're actually ready to depart. But the pelvic region needs attention throughout our entire lifetimes. Since the pelvis is the center of all movement and balance, it can be the greatest asset for enhancing longevity when it is strong because movements that originate here help strengthen muscle, bone and connective tissue. But when the pelvis is frail, it becomes our "Achilles' heel," with the most dangerous repercussions when it breaks.

As we get older, there's a bigger difference in appearance and lifestyle between those of us who cultivate strength and "pelvic power" and those who do not. One woman's meat, so to speak, becomes another one's poison. A robust older woman can continue to hike, dance, ride bikes, etc., indefinitely and without much fear. But a frail woman who does such things is at a much higher risk of losing her balance, falling and therefore fracturing a hip. A robust older woman might do a lifetime of stomach crunches to "tone her abs." But if a frail woman does this, she could easily fracture a vertebra in her spine.

Although the bone-degenerating disease osteoporosis becomes most apparent after women go through menopause, it is, according to Dr. Frank Bonner of the National Osteoporosis Foundation, "a pediatric disease with a geriatric outcome." In other words, we lay the groundwork for this disease with inactivity in youth. But we make it worse with:

- lifelong inactivity

- chronic dieting

- drinking too much coffee and caffeinated diet sodas

- smoking cigarettes

- taking birth control pills

- and *excessive* exercise, especially when it interrupts the menstrual cycle.

These are some of the risk factors we can control. The risk factors we can't control include being:

- Caucasian

- Asian

- prematurely gray

- small boned and/or thin

- in a family with a history of osteoporosis.

Carrying "extra" body weight can actually help prevent osteoporosis since additional weight exerts greater force on bones, thus making them stronger. But large, unfit women get osteoporosis, too.

According to a federal study, osteoporosis-related fractures were the *sixth leading cause of death* among the elderly (mostly women) and resulted in *ten billion dollars* in annual medical costs (and growing every year)! Women aren't the only ones who get osteoporosis. Seventy-five percent of all men over seventy-five are at risk. But, for women, our introduction into our "osteoporosis years" is much more pronounced—and it sprouts as we enter our "wise years," just when we need the support of a strong body to house our blooming spirits.

The two leading causes of osteoporosis—lack of strength due to lifelong inactivity and insufficient calcium—are reversible! Even after menopause, when the damage would seem to have been done, taking calcium and exercising regularly *can* thicken bones, but only when done together. In other words, simply exercising or taking 1,000 to 1,500 milligrams of calcium a day alone won't do it. They only work in tandem.

Women need "weight-bearing" exercise. In other words, we need to exert gravity or an extra force on our muscles as when we walk, dance or lift weights. Water exercise *isn't* weight bearing, and so women shouldn't look to achieve all exercise benefits from the water (although there's some debate about water exercise's ability to thicken bones). Water exercise is a great complementary exercise, and wonderful for healing. But ideally, we all need some land-based exercise because we don't live in the water.

Once serious bone degeneration has set in (something that can be determined from a bone-scan test), the main goal of any older woman's exercise routine shouldn't be making bones strong but preventing *fractures* by preventing falls. The best way to do this is to strengthen the pelvic stabilizers. Some of the simplest activities that do this are Tai Chi, walking, weight lifting or yoga. But one of the most thorough, effective and *enjoyable* ways to do this is with dancing moves and exercises that highlight the pelvis. (In chapter 7, moves that specifically enhance "pelvic power" are marked with a *P*.) It is also a good idea, particularly as we get older, to help prevent falls by tying up loose electrical cords, doing away with slippery throw rugs, lighting dark walkways, etc. But the very *best* way to prevent osteoporosis-related problems is to start young and continue with regular physical activities which strengthen bones and the muscles that govern balance.

The Magic Well

The pelvis is the passageway between spirit and flesh. Thousands of years ago, humans made the connection between pelvis and spirit and believed that the pelvis was the "divine receiver" of life energy. Thus, the pelvis earned its name "sacrum" which translates into "sacred bone." It was con-

"Coiled at the base of the spine lies the serpent power, kundalini . . . the great pristine force which underlies all organic and inorganic matter. As the individual develops it uncoils and rises from the realms of darkness below to the light and spirit above."

—DAVID TANSLEY, *Subtle Body, Essence and Shadow*

"Although to Western minds, chi would be a type of bio-energy, the Taoist chi is equivalent to what is known as the soul, and is an air or breath energy considered to be feminine in its action . . . It originates in the burst of energy released during the sexual act of our own conception and dissipates continuously through our lives."

—A.T. MANN AND JANE LYLE, *Sacred Sexuality*

sidered "the gateway of life" because it was believed that through this passage we not only conceived and birthed our children, but we also received our own life energy. Many believed that what first brought us into being was an explosion of energy at the end of our mother's umbilicus. Our navel centers, they believed, then held the reservoir of that original life force. Thus, preserving that supply grew to be of tantamount importance. If we did not replenish this energy pool, people believed our life would dribble out. But, they also believed that if we replenished that energy with attention and right actions, we could not only preserve it but also generate it and circulate it around our bodies.

Some of the best ways to do this, they believed, were through activities like dance, Tai Chi, yoga, sexuality combined with love and spiritual devotion, meditation, deep breathing, fresh water and food, being out in Nature breathing fresh air and choosing a positive outlook over negativity. Many of these activities have pelvic connections.

In matriarchal cultures, the pelvis was the "throne of the Goddess." In the Indian Tantric tradition, the pelvis was home of "kundalini," the coiled serpent of spirit which could rise when sexual energy was guided with a yogic, meditative discipline. "Kundalini" draws from the root word "kunda" which means reservoir or pool. It is also believed to be dangerous when allowed to run excessively "hot and wild." In Chinese Taoist practices, the pelvic-abdominal region is home to the "tan tien," "a radiating ball of light" about the size of a fist. Practitioners of martial arts and meditation consider this *the* center of all energy and movement.

This is also home to the first three "chakras." "Chakras" are believed to be wheel-shaped, flowerlike funnels of energy, which take in "life energy" and distribute it to the closest nerves and organs. They have no physical manifestation; at least Western science hasn't proved they exist. But it is believed that these first three chakras are our most "embodied" energy centers, governing sexuality, survival, emotions, and how we regard ourselves and relate to others. It is believed that the four higher chakras govern our reach toward higher consciousness. But without the pelvis providing an earthy foundation for our energy and more basic instincts, spirit has no place to plant its roots.

It's hard to look even briefly at the movement and meditative practices that have grown up around the sacrum and then look back at our hips in the same old way. Yes, our hips balance groceries, laundry and children, get tamed in girdles and beaten into submission with leg lifts, squats and machines. But the pelvis has long held a place of honor in the spiritual history of humanity, especially the spiritual history of women. Perhaps, then, on an unconscious level we *understand* the sacred nature of the sacred bone and that is why we tattoo birds and butterflies across this part of our bodies. Perhaps that is why it hurts so much to hear women say we "hate our hips." The pelvis stores the magic we can extract from our spirit-bodies, if we're simply willing to take the time to feel it there and lovingly coax it to expand. Through the pelvis, we can discover our divinity and even rebirth ourselves.

6 Patterns of Wholeness

For years I'd been "searching for my dance" but didn't realize what I'd been doing. When I landed upon the four shapes outlined in this chapter—the circle, figure 8, spiral and snake—I started dancing with a pleasure, precision and spontaneous freedom I had never experienced up to that point. I "found" my dance, or perhaps let it find me.

Finding the Dance

"Zigzags, wavy lines, and interlocking spirals, common features of Paleolithic and Neolithic art, represent the waters of life, the cosmic deep from which all life springs."

—MARIA GIMBUTAS, *The Goddesses and Gods of Old Europe*

I soon discovered that others could benefit from these shapes since they are simple, universal, easy to visualize and, to some extent, easy to reproduce as well. Thus, it seemed that everyone could use them to find their own dances. These shapes provided the foundation for free-flowing movement, proper alignment and individual style. They could be kept basic and repetitive or spun into countless variations. They heightened the "feminine" abilities to sense and be spontaneous and provided the "masculine" concepts of structure and accuracy. But more important, even women who once claimed they "could never move like that," had "no rhythm," or "two left feet" were suddenly able to dance in a way that felt natural and made them look beautiful.

To make sure I wasn't just dancing on my own ecstatic cloud, however,

I took each movement presented in this book and ran it through a test. To satisfy the "masculine" principles of reason and science, the answer to each of these questions had to be yes:

- "Is this an intelligent way to do this—and if so, can I say why?"

- "Is it safe?"

- "Does it enhance aerobic conditioning, strength and/or flexibility?"

- "Does this qualify as 'a workout'?"

- "Will it help burn fat?"

- "Will it give positive, visible results?"

- "Will it *serve* (rather than damage) the body in the long run—especially an older body?"

- "Can this work for others, especially those intimidated by dance?"

To stay true to the "feminine" principles of "sensing" and providing pleasure, each movement also had to inspire a "yes" to these questions:

- "Is it fun?"

- "Is it aesthetically pleasing?"

- "Does it lift the spirit?"

- "Does it feel comfortable?"

- "Do I lose track of time as I do this?"

- "Do I stop worrying about 'getting results' while I get them?"

- "Does it put me in harmony with who I am or yearn to be?"

- "Does this make other dancers happy, too?"

Each move passed the tests, so there is a balance of masculine and feminine and, as you will see, also right and left brain. The result is whole-brain functioning and whole-body dancing.

Right Brain, Left Brain and Two Left Feet

"Form is the envelope of pulsation."

—ANCIENT TANTRIC WISDOM

Moving is a whole-brain experience. But the way some people move, you wouldn't know it. Each side of the brain actually dominates movements on the body's other side. Right brain rules left side. Left brain rules right side. Stroke victims, for example, who lose brain capacity on one side, are often paralyzed down the other half of the body. Many beginner dance, aerobics or even walking students seem to have just one side of the brain in operation as well and will often simultaneously lift the *same* arm and leg. (Try it. It's hard.) The nonworking side of the brain actually goes quiet to accommodate such a lopsided, unnatural moving style. Using the *opposite* arm and leg at the same time (especially when movements cross the center line of the body) brings both halves of the brain into play.

Many of us acquire movement *personalities* that favor one side of the brain as well. People who prefer rational, left-brain (predominantly "masculine") movements like:

- very precise choreography

- structured counts

- moving in sync with a group

- following the leader

- clear beginnings, middles and ends

- precise rhythms and moving on the beat

- facing the mirror

- *not* being singled out to perform for others

People who prefer spatially sensitive right-brain (predominantly "feminine") movements enjoy:

- formless, free expression

- dancing alone, unchained by a group or choreography

- changeable rhythms and moving against the beat

- dancing away from the mirror

- dancing in front of an audience, revealing their "essence"

Both right- and left-brain moving styles have their place. Left-brain movements take us from point A to point B and help us follow a sequence in a group. Right-brain movements add the sensitivity, emotion and spatial awareness that give dance its passion and placement. But in both dance and the real world, it's ideal to have a balance of the two.

In her book *Drawing on the Right Side of the Brain* (Tarcher/Putnam, 1989), Betty Edwards shows dramatically different results when a beginning student draws a chair first from the logical left side of the brain and later from the right. Ms. Edwards states that when we use our left brains, we draw a *symbol* of the chair and its parts, not the chair itself. We draw with our "grown-up" rational mind that likes to categorize things. (Our right and left hemispheres actually split into two distinct halves, with separate functions, sometime around age ten. Not coincidentally, that's the age when we start to judge our drawings and, therefore, often stop drawing altogether. Thus, our drawing ability suffers from "arrested development."[1] Our dance ability can suffer the same fate.) The left brain hears the assignment "Draw a chair" and doesn't draw what it *sees*, but what it *knows* the chair contains: seat, back, legs, etc. The drawing ends up looking very childish, with no perspective. In other words, because our left brain likes to label and figure things out in advance, it actually distorts our ability to *see*. On top of that, it judges its work harshly, gets frustrated and gives up.

With our right brains, however, we can see the seemingly random squiggles of space *around* the chair. It's much easier to draw nameless shapes than to "draw a chair." But to use the right-brain skills, we have to trick the left brain into quieting down. It's not unlike distracting a pesky child. To do this, we just have to keep focusing on the nameless shapes. Once we hear ourselves think "ugh-oh, this is the arm of the chair. I can't draw this" we have to refocus on the nameless, negative space around the chair. (Ms. Edwards also recommends that we get a picture of something we want to draw, turn it upside down and draw it from that perspective. This also turns the subject into a collection of nameless shapes.) Thus, we break through our self-judgment and limited understanding of what chairs are *supposed*

[1]Betty Edwards, *Drawing on the Right Side of the Brain* (New York: Tarcher/Putnam, 1989; originally published in 1976), 59.

to look like and, much to our amazement, draw a chair! This same process can also happen with dance. It's less intimidating to follow the assignment "Draw a circle with your tailbone" than it is to learn a complicated routine or perform steps with fancy names. When we keep it this simple, then everyone can be a dancer.

In *A Woman's Book of Strength*, I wrote about "drawing with weights." Every exercise, when broken down, became a semicircle or straight line, depending on how many joints were involved in a movement. By using simple visuals like these, I taught myself and others how to lift weights correctly with an intelligent use of both muscles and gravity. This also revealed the underlying geometry that linked all exercises and therefore made them easier to learn. In this book, I'm presenting four familiar shapes that we draw *with our bodies*. Whether we focus on drawing the space *around* the shape or draw the shape itself, the result is the same because drawing with the body is much more vague than using pen and paper; it takes an "inner eye." This immediately accesses the right hemisphere, which is very comfortable combining geometrical shapes with movement and imagination.

Most movement classes employ more of a left-brain approach. Facing the mirror, following the teacher, counting, learning complicated choreography, anticipating what's coming next and worrying about how we look are left-brain activities. All these can trip the feet and dull the sensors that create spontaneous, coordinated, natural movement. The easiest way to quiet the left brain while dancing is to turn away from the mirror, close our eyes or soften our focus, listen closely to the music, don't look at anyone else, simply choose to ignore anyone who might be watching us (this takes a little practice) and engage the imagination in "making shapes," or use the shapes to evoke emotion or tell a story. A simple shape gives enough concrete form to satisfy the left-brain mover and enough opportunity for variation and self-expression to satisfy the right-brain mover.

For many of us, however, moving with a right-brain approach incites terror. We feel safe following a group and watching our reflections even if we don't like what we see. But putting all the focus "out there" on the group or the mirror often robs us of the experience "in here" in our bodies.

The mirror is especially seductive. Yes, it can be a useful learning tool, but many dancers become addicted to it. In the musical *A Chorus Line*, Cassie sings, "All I ever needed was the music and the mirror." It mesmerizes. It can reflect reality or fantasy. But there comes a point when we have to turn away from it so we can put our attention on what we're doing. Although we may feel ripped away from our reflections at first, it only takes a few moments to be weaned. When I teach a class, I'm fairly sneaky about this. I teach a warm-up and perhaps a few dances facing the mirror and then, using the formula and some of the ideas in "More Food for the Right Brain" presented in this chapter, have everyone turn away and "draw shapes," safe in the solitude of their own space. Or I'll have everyone pick up simple percussive instruments so they can heighten their listening and, therefore, rhythmic dancing skills. When our other senses are engaged, the mirror doesn't facilitate dancing; it interrupts it. When our other senses are engaged, we not only learn faster; we also discover *how* we learn. We switch from followers into individuals.

Sometimes at the end of class, I bring us together in a circle. Those who want to perform can dance inside the circle in the ancient tradition of women dancing for one another. Those who do not can sit and watch. As a teacher, it gives me tremendous joy to watch "nondancers" and "secret dancers" not only dancing but also eager to perform.

This doesn't mean that one or two sessions of shape making turns everyone into "dancers." There is still the purely physical side of muscle and motion. It takes time for muscles to figure out how much force to use and therefore adapt to these new demands by creating greater strength, endurance and flexibility. At the beginning of any new movement venture, there's always a learning curve for body and mind. During the unskilled phase, movements tend to take more energy. Witness the difference between someone just learning how to swim and an accomplished swimmer. The beginner flails, splashes and wears herself out in just a few strokes. But the accomplished swimmer glides like a dolphin and can keep going for a long time, barely kicking up a splash. Unskilled movers also tend to make jerky and uncoordinated movements. Skill brings fluidity and efficiency. When the moves are already fluid to begin with, however, it takes less time to achieve mastery. Ironically, mastery will also come sooner to those who are willing to slow down and "sense" their way through movement than to those who are worried about getting results and looking good.

We learn movement by repetition and rhythm. If we break a movement down to very simple elements—one shape, one body part or one basic step—we learn very quickly, usually in an average of eight to thirty-two counts. One move contains a world of variations and opportunities to truly

"In art (the Goddess) is manifested by the signs of dynamic motion: whirling and twisting spirals, winding and coiling snakes, circles, crescents, horns, sprouting seeds and shoots."

—MARIA GIMBUTAS, *The Language of the Goddess*

dissect, feel, understand. It's more important to learn the value of one move and mine it for its emotional possibilities than to impress ourselves or others with a huge vocabulary of "tricks." Movement skills are also cumulative. Once we successfully perform one movement—and really know it down to our bones, that movement skill, like riding a bicycle, is always ours to enjoy.

Research?

"The spiral tendency within each one of us is the longing for and growth towards wholeness."

—JILL PURCE,
The Mystic Spiral, Journey of the Soul

When I began researching the subject of soft, rounded moves versus linear and sharp ones and their effects on muscles, joints, moods, etc. I found almost no studies that had looked into this subject. Scientific studies deal in measurable results: amount of energy expended, weight lifted, distance covered at various speeds, etc. As far as I know, there are no instruments delicate enough to measure "movement quality" and how it affects our psyches, spirits, sense of space, perception of our bodies, whether it causes anxiety or well-being or to what degree it inspires integrated, whole-brain function. I'm left to go by my own experiences which say that rounded motions feel better than straight ones, make us strong in otherwise hard-to-reach muscles, keep us limber and lean, make us feel beautiful, inspire mental satisfaction and lend a spiritual resonance. More women leave the room smiling. Who needs a machine to measure that?

But I still felt compelled to find scientific data to support my belief and prove to myself and the more scientifically inclined that I'm not completely out of my mind. The only research I found, however, was on related subjects.

• The American College of Sports Medicine has revised its exercise recommendations to include *moderate* (as opposed to "vigorous") aerobic exercise three days a week for thirty minutes to maintain cardiovascular health. Their definition of moderate was "brisk walking." But soft, round dancing can certainly fit into that category since a dancer can control her level of exertion (for that same reason, she can make it more vigorous if she craves more intensity). Many surveys revealed that "inactive people" avoid exercise because it seems *too* vigorous. Moderate exercise, however, is easier to maintain and enjoy—and could in fact be better for us in the long run since it involves "less risk of injuries to ligaments, tendons, muscles and bones" while still providing beneficial effects on "blood pressure, lipid metabolism (especially increases in high-density cholesterol) . . . "[2] This isn't to say that vigorous is bad if we're conditioned enough to handle it. But the reality is that the majority of us will only choose between moderate exercise or nothing at all.

• A study out of Washington University School of Medicine in St. Louis, led by Dr. Michael Province, compared the effects of Tai Chi and more traditional Western exercise (weight training, walking, jogging, stretching, etc.) on balance in the elderly. This study found that Tai Chi reduced the risk of falling by twenty-five percent—almost twice as much as Western exercise! Tai Chi's slow, controlled movements involve sinking weight down into the legs and shifting weight (something that I incorporate into both my warm-up and dancing). What the study did *not* address was the role that *concentration* plays in aiding balance. Incidentally, both Tai Chi and soft, rounded dancing promote mental focus and cultivate "chi." But the study didn't mention that, either. Chi falls into the category of the "unmeasurable."

• Deborah Kerns, from Texas Women's University, in Denton, Texas, did the only study I've seen on the *psychological* effects of different types of aerobic dance classes.[3] She compared standard aerobics classes (based on guidelines from the American Council on Exercise) and "NIA," (Neuromuscular Integrative Action), the love and brainchild of Debbie and Carlos Rosas of Portland, Oregon. NIA is a dance-fitness methodology that integrates moves from various types of dance, martial arts, yoga, Feldenkrais, Alexander work and deep abdominal breathing—all time-tested techniques for well-being. (For more information on NIA, see p. 179.) Ms. Kerns points out that standard aerobic programs haven't emphasized well-being as much as "discipline, self-restraint, denial and external control." This approach to health has inspired "excessive exercise, rising incidents of eating disorders and the promotion of thinness as a standard of body attractiveness as a panacea for life's difficulties." In her study seventy-seven women followed a seven-week program, twice a week for an hour, half in the standard class and half in the NIA classes. Although both types of classes promoted general self-esteem, those in the standard classes

[2]William L. Haskell, Ph.D., "Resolving the Exercise Debate: More vs. Less," *Idea Today* (October 1995), 42.
[3]D. Kerns, "A Comparison of a Mind/Body Approach versus a Conventional Approach to Aerobic Dance" 7-1 *Women's Health Issues* (Jan.–Feb. 1997), Jacob's Institute of Women's Health, New York, N.Y.

reported feeling " 'rushed' when class was over, 'guilty' if they ate a fattening food and 'stressed to keep up with everyone else.' " Those in the NIA group reported feeling " 'less stressed,' 'relaxed,' 'calm' when class was over, and they had learned to 'use the breathing techniques' whenever they felt angry or stressed outside of class." The in-class experience for the standard group was "stressed to keep up with everyone else, incompetent, uncoordinated, struggling," while the NIA group reported feelings of "joy, hope, appreciation for my body, moving freely, rejuvenation, power and grace."

> "In the sacred dance we mirror the microcosmic order of the heavens, the gyratory movements representing the whirling of the stars above the fixed earth. As we wind, we create within ourselves a still center and apprehend the universe into being; as we unwind, we turn our spirit back to its divine state."
>
> —COURTNEY DAVIS, *The Celtic Arts Sourcebook*

The above research shows that we're headed in the right direction, toward an integration of body, spirit and mind to achieve not just fitness but inner-outer health. This evolution in fitness involves a merging of Western and Eastern practices, ancient and "cutting edge," intuitive and rational. More and more of us are hungry, if not starved, for such satisfaction. We're led to this by instinct, without an overwhelming amount of scientific proof, simply because scientists haven't yet invented the machinery powerful or delicate enough to measure what is still unmeasurable. In the meantime, the best choice is to keep dancing, keep looking back to what the ancients used to cultivate body wisdom and moving forward, so we can integrate such practices into our modern lives. Instincts and intuition, after all, are the most powerful tools of the Divine Feminine.

Sacred Geometry—The Four Shapes

> "To ask what a spiral pattern means is like asking what does music mean?"
>
> —AIDAN MEEHAN, *Celtic Design, Spiral Patterns*

What makes any shape or space sacred is the meaning we bring to it. Yet certain shapes and spaces seem to resonate with more power and affect us in more profound ways than others, whether we find sacred meaning in them or not. A rounded room, a circle of stones, a group seated in a circle all have a different impact on our senses than a room full of hard edges, objects lined up in straight neat lines or a classroom with desks all in a row. When we make shapes with our *bodies*, the impact is even more profound, since our flesh and bones not only *become* the shapes but take on their characteristics. Quick linear motions send much different messages to the body and brain than soft, rounded shapes do. Hard, linear moves feel like fighting. With them we cut through space, define or conquer it. They can be dramatic to watch but also produce anxiety in the audience and the dancer. Soft, rounded motions feel like caresses. With them we curl through space and simply move around any obstacles. Curving movements are pleasing to watch and have a hypnotic effect on the dancer and the observer. They're also more conducive to inspiring a sense of the sacred, since they put the dancer in a less aggressive, more receptive state. Since the following shapes have appeared in artwork from virtually every major civilization, it is no surprise that they are also already loaded with history and symbolic meaning.

THE CIRCLE

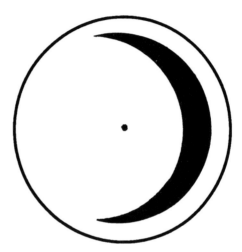

Lacking a beginning and end, **THE CIRCLE** is unchanging, unbroken, a symbol of heavenly perfection, wholeness, the womb, the wheel of life, death and rebirth; it is the Sun, the Moon, the Earth, the Great Goddess, the Universal Mother. Its membrane both protects those within it and excludes those without. It is, like the Goddess, complete unto itself and needs nothing. Its center symbolizes the infinite still point, the nucleus within the vast cosmic whole. The dancer has a similar still point, a center from which all motions spring. But the circle also contains energy swirling inside its circumference, just as we do.

As dancers, we're always contained inside our own invisible, circular bubbles. Just like Leonardo da Vinci's famous "Universal Man," whose two pairs of arms and legs touch the inside edge of an orb, our circle ends at our fingers and toes. We take this circle with us wherever we move.

Dances that celebrate life and death are often done in a circle to honor the cyclical nature of seasons, the cycle of life. Dancing in the round also gives unity to the dancers who face one another. It's an equalizing geometry because, in it, no one is placed above or below anyone else.

Both crescents (open circles) and ovals (flattened circles) are cousins of the circle. Big circles can also house little circles inside them.

THE FIGURE 8

THE FIGURE 8 is really two circles (or ovals) touching or intersecting heads, with a charged central point where the two sides meet. Its symmetrical sides both symbolize perfect balance, as well as duality—the creative and destructive, full and empty, dark and light, masculine and feminine, right and left, opposing and unified. Like the symbol for yin and yang, each side reflects the other, with a spot of the other's color within. Like the circle, the boundary of the figure 8 is complete and continuous and always returns back to itself; thus it signifies infinity. Where the circles intersect an almond-shaped design is formed, which in Hindu mythology is called a "mandorla." This has also been called the "womb of Chaos, the womb of the Goddess of the night, and the mouth that speaks the word of creation."[4]

[4]Michael Schneider, *A Beginner's Guide to Constructing the Universe. A Voyage from 1 to 10* (New York: Harper Perennial, 1994), 32.

The figure 8 first separates, then unifies both sides of the body into one. To fully master both halves of the figure 8, the dancer must individually dissect and understand each side. Beginners usually have more trouble mastering one side of a figure 8 than the other. Sometimes this is purely physical. One side is tighter than the other and just needs attention before it will loosen up. Many dancers also say they discover a "blip" in their brains where the two halves don't seem to match or connect. But with practice, this gap is bridged and the figure 8 becomes as full on one side as the other.

Once full symmetry is achieved, it's fun to vary the symmetrical shape and consciously give the figure 8 a big head on one side, a small one on the other. Figure 8's are most commonly danced with hips, rib cage and shoulders and arms.

THE SPIRAL

THE SPIRAL is one of nature's most common forms of growth. Teeth, trees, animal horns, fingernails all grow this way. The spiral is self-referential. As it grows, it keeps making larger patterns of itself in a kind of homage to the original. Ancient people believed that both physical and spiritual energy flowed in spirals. Today, many still believe this is true, that chakras, for instance, both draw in and expel energy in spiraling wheels. The kundalini cobra also spirals up through the chakras and up the spine, ascending from raw, unrefined power into etheric and heavenly prana. The spiral is determined not just by the form itself, but also by the "negative" space between each segment. Thus, it is a symbol of the seen and unseen, the female and male and the unity between two "opposing forces," traveling together like two unlikely companions, committed to reaching an unknown end.

To move in a spiral is to expand or contract, to spin away from the center or return to it. To spiral outward is to evolve and embark on a journey. To spiral in is to contract and come back home. We learn in a spiraling fashion: learning, absorbing, forgetting, relearning, processing again.

Spins that start small and expand out or start big and curl in tight both employ the spiral. Any circular motions that move away from a center point in any direction essentially become spirals. Spiral turns are different from pirouettes, which revolve around a fixed axis, spinning, like a top, in place.

THE SNAKE

THE SNAKE is a highly charged symbol with a lingering bad reputation. It's difficult, particularly for modern, Western people to look beyond the

---

Garden of Eden, the phallic symbol and general fear of reptiles to see the beauty even within the *symbol* of snakes, let alone the animal. In Goddess cultures, snakes represented the power of the Earth, because their bellies caressed it when they moved, also because snakes possessed the ability to shed their skins—a symbol of the cycle of life and regeneration—the very skill possessed by the Sacred Feminine. Snakes represented a watery, boneless quality, the undulation of waves, the ability to nurture life in warm dampness, as women do in our wombs. But they also represented the unification of both male and female sexuality contained within one form, the self-fertilizing virgin mother, the omni or bisexual, the woman who needs no man. No wonder a woman with a snake is a potent, intimidating symbol. Statues of snakes and snake goddesses appeared all over the world. The famous statue of the Minoan snake goddess/priestess (which dates back to 1600 B.C. from the palace of Knossos in Crete), shows her eyes wide, her body voluptuous, her whole being "charged" with the power of the snakes in her hands.

The serpent has long represented the power of mystics. The kundalini cobra is not the only one. The snake appears in old woodcuts of alchemists who tried to turn base metal into gold. To alchemists, snakes represented the primal wisdom of the Earth (from which base metals come). With this raw energy, they hoped to combine consciously directed (sexual?) energy and create actual or metaphorical gold.

The power of the snake is also found on the caduceus, the symbol of the medical profession. The caduceus features two snakes wrapped around a sword. The Greek god Hermes (the Roman god Mercury) supposedly threw a sword between two fighting snakes, who then stopped fighting and coiled up the staff together; thus, this symbol came to represent peace, harmony, health and the concept that Nature has the power to heal itself (a concept that is sadly often lost in Western medicine). In some representations, these two snakes on the caduceus are connected at the base in one body. The caduceus also mimics the same shape of the double helix of DNA, the ultimate "patterns of wholeness" which determine our genetic individuality.

The snake didn't earn its evil reputation until the Garden of Eden. It's not surprising that this feminine symbol of the Goddess was turned into a symbol of evil, since the pagan goddesses and gods were considered evil. Later of course, the snake came to be a symbol of male potency because of its obvious similarity to a penis, a point that was hammered into us by Sigmund Freud.

Since snakes represent everything that slithers including our own sexuality, it's not surprising that snaking movements have long been interpreted as sensual, sexual, evil. Of all the shapes listed here, snaking undulations require the most exquisite body control and are perhaps most beautiful to watch. Snaking moves are actually open-ended figure 8's. In other words, the rippling motion flows *through* the body without folding back on itself, as if happening *to* us. Thus many people observing "snaking dancers" have thought them to be possessed or in a trance. Is it any wonder, then, that snaking moves have long been regarded as suggestive, indecent, the kind of things that have inspired lust and violence in observers and have damned dancers to hell? It is true, however, that to allow the full power of the snake to pass through the body, we must surrender to it, ride the wave.

The snake is found not just in "snake arms" but also in torso undulations or body waves. A snake, moving very fast, becomes a shimmy.

The Dance Formula:
Drawing with Your Body—Take One from Column A . . .

The best way to approach this movement formula is to keep it simple. Take any of the shapes from Column A and draw them with the various body parts in Column B. While you're reading, draw a random invisible line from Column A to Column B to create a pair (i.e., figure 8's and tailbone). Now, imagine what sort of movements might follow . . .

COLUMN A — SHAPES	COLUMN B — BODY PARTS
circles	feet
figure 8's	legs
spirals	tailbone, hips
snake	spinal column
	chest/rib cage
	shoulders/elbows/wrists

(Avoid using the neck, except for half circles to the front. Drawing with the head can make you dizzy and hurt the upper part of your spine. Keep your head aligned on your spine.)

To create a logical sequence, you can begin with one body part, for instance, shoulders:

1. Draw circles (and, if you're so inclined, their variations: big circles, little circles, half circles, circles within circles, reverse directions, etc.).

2. Then draw figure 8's (and their variations: symmetrical and nonsymmetrical shapes).

3. Move on to spirals (draw a spiral with shoulders and arms or allow your body to complete the spiral by turning).

4. And then draw the snake (move from slow undulations to shimmies).

After you've finished with shoulders, try the same sequencing with rib cage. Move through the body either going from:

1. head to toe

2. toe to head or

3. start with hips, spine, rib cage to warm big muscles first so that heat radiates out to limbs. Then add feet, legs, shoulders and arms.

Some body parts respond better to certain shapes than to others. But it's worth exploring them all since you never know what you'll discover.

Column C, Your Canvas . . .

Draw not only in the air around you but think of all the hard surfaces of the room as your canvas:

- the floor

- the walls (front, side and back)

- the ceiling

Or put them all together and draw on the floor, up one wall, on the ceiling and down the other wall, mimicking the motion of

- a wheel.

Imagine that every movement leaves a mark on your canvas. Become aware of the true dimensions of your shapes. Are your circles round or elliptical? Are your figure 8's symmetrical or not? Drawing the original shape true to form is less important than drawing the shape you *intend* to draw. Think of shapes as the colors on your palette, the body parts your brushes. The quality of your movement determines the thickness, delicacy or steady "hand" of your strokes.

As you'll see in the next chapter, these shapes work both as a warm-up and as a structure for the dance. But whether you're warming up or dancing, try to repeat a distinct shape with a repetitive rhythm until you feel that it's "imprinted" into your body's memory before spinning off into variations.

This will give your muscles and joints time enough to "lubricate" and adapt to the movement but will also provide you with feedback about your personality. Notice if you like to explore a shape for a long time (i.e., have right-brained tendencies) or feel bored after just a few seconds (left-brained tendencies). Do the variations seem to come on their own (right brain) or do you *think* about what to do next (left brain)? Once you identify your personality, try exploring the opposite. If you're quickly bored, stay with a shape *longer* than eight repetitions to see if you can discover subtleties beyond the obvious. This might go against everything in your nature at first, but it's good medicine for expanding mental limits.

This type of movement works best with music that isn't "beat-dominant." The music can be steadily rhythmic but the rhythm shouldn't *demand* you follow it, the way a disco beat can. Arrhythmic, melodic music works well, too. The music should lift your spirit and inspire motion. Listen for the off beats, the down beats and other irregularities and work those into your dance. Once you can do these things, then any music will do—Beethoven, Elvis, Bo-Diddley, Sheryl Crow.

Once you feel comfortable with the shapes and their variations, start playing with different tempos. Tempo choices depend on the music and the rhythms you hear inside the music. (If this is too much to think about, don't worry about it. Choosing tempos is fairly automatic). Nonetheless, your choices are these:

Column D, Tempos

Steady:
  Slow
  Moderate
  Fast
Variable:
  Crescendos from slow to fast (and perhaps back to slow). Also the reverse.
  Constantly changing (what I call "scat dancing")

Slow, controlled movements are probably the toughest to perform and create a hypnotic feel—a bit like walking through clouds. Steady, moderate tempos provide a useful base when you want to add a variety of tempos. Unadorned, however, they can appear clean or dull, depending on the dancer and dance. Fast tempos can take you on a wild ride. To keep control even when speeding, remember to use your center.

Although the point of this section is to present a rounded movement style that complements your womanly body and sense of the sacred, I'm not saying you can't add a straight line, walk from point A to B or punctuate a movement with a clean line or jab. But remember that soft lines, circles and spins don't exact as big a toll on your joints, generate more ability and grace and can keep you dancing longer.

More Food for the Right Brain

• Add *feeling* to your movements. Notice how your heart feels when the chest is wide open—and how it feels when it's protected and closed. Use those emotions to spice up your dance.

• Respect your body's signals and respond when it asks you to slow down or repeat something it didn't understand.

• Come in as a clean slate every time. Each day, each dance is an opportunity to create anew. Avoid judging today's ability against another's. Avoid trying to repeat a past performance.

• Treat each song as a separate entity. Acknowledge its beginning, middle and end. As an exercise in discipline, don't stop dancing until the song is through.

• Dance completely *against* the tide of a song. If it's a fast song, dance slowly. If it's slow, use quick movements. If it's got uneven rhythms, dance smoothly. If it's melodic and even tempered, make movements restless and ambitious.

• Fall in love with the details. Find rapture in the subtle exchange between your body and the music. Play your muscles as different instruments in a symphony orchestra.

• Use adjectives and adverbs to inspire your dance. Think textures: "jagged, silky, crisp." Think action: "meandering, pulsing, still." Don't act out the words. Use them instead to paint your internal landscape. I find this much easier than dancing interpretations of very large concepts like "wind," "a growing tree," "fire" or "the ocean" as we used to in modern dance class.

• Use clear visual and sensual actions you can act out. Think of: shaping a clay pot on a wheel, letting your fingers wave like silk in a breeze, breaking out of a small box and emerging into a lush landscape, drinking from a well of wisdom.

• Try dancing in different (but safe) places. Dance in a clearing in the woods. Dance in a park, on the beach or on your back porch. Wear armor (and headphones) against other people's judgment, envy or embarrassment. And always carry spare batteries!

More Sacred Geometry

This last bit of sacred geometry is about orientation; i.e., clearly marking the space you're dancing *in*. Whether you're alone in a room, in class or onstage, these shapes help you hone your focus and direction, which helps you better communicate your dance to others (present or absent) or to yourself. The following shapes are all contained within a circle because we dance inside our own circles as well.

Column E, Direction

1. The line inside the circle (or polar opposites)

2. Triangle within a circle (point up and point down)

3. Square and cross within a circle

4. Pentacle (five-pointed star) within a circle

5. Six-pointed star (or two triangles) within a circle

Most of the floors and stages we dance on are square. But even on a square surface, dancing inside a circle works well because the edges of most rectangular floors are far from the center of the action. If you're on-stage and stray into the corners, you may literally find yourself in the dark.

The more directions you choose to address, the greater the complexity—and with too many directions, it's easy to lose focus. That's why I haven't mentioned more than six directions. Like the first four shapes, these geometric shapes also contain an ancient, archetypal history, which is especially interesting to know when you're creating a ritual dance or ceremony. But they're also useful for blocking space.

THE LINE or polar opposite is the simplest of directions but also the least evolved. It's north and south, east and west, black and white, heaven and hell. If you can only move front and back or side to side, you may feel like a rat pacing in a cage. The straight line is clean but sexless—a ruler's edge, a teeter-totter. Running from side to side, a dancer appears confused.

THE TRIANGLE represents the Triple Goddess and the Trinity. In Goddess cultures it was the Maiden, Mother, Crone; in patriarchal religions, the Father, Son and Holy Ghost. Three also represents body, mind, spirit/birth, life, death/past, present, future. Typically, when the triangle point is down this represents the female sex organ, as well as the female principle, grace descending, heavenly guidance being received from above. When the point is up, it represents the masculine, with energy pointed upward and sent to Heaven.

THE SQUARE is a symbol of man-made perfection. Its four corners stand for reason, completion, stability and balanced, earthly order. Its solidity is substantial. A big square building seems massively reassuring somehow, although not necessarily pleasing to look at unless it is decorated with arches and curves or some other softening enhancements. The square also symbolizes the four elements (fire, earth, water, air), the four directions (north, south, east, west) and the four limbs, the squared balance of the human body. As humans we depend on the square to measure our seasons, square our construction, do dealings that are "fair and square" and look others square in the eye. It's highly useful, functional and arithmetically correct. Ask any builder. It's much easier to build a square structure than a circular one. To the dancer, the square marks the typical manner in which space is divided. Too often, inside a square, the space feels limited, too small and full of other bodies.

THE CROSS is the square without a border. It contains the linear comfort of ninety-degree angles yet isn't as confining as the square because it isn't closed in. The cross has been a potent symbol not just for Christians but in many other religions as well: the (pagan) Celtic cross, the Egyptian ankh, the Rosicrucian "rosy cross," even the swastika (really a spinning cross) which was a Buddhist and Hindu symbol before Hitler appropriated it. The cross is a symbol of unity between the Divine (the vertical line) and the human (the horizontal). The body at the center of the cross symbolizes divine energy made manifest in human form.

The cross is useful to the dancer because it points out the four directions, while keeping the dancer at the intersection. Both the cross and the square, however, can get tediously predictable: front, back, side, side. To make it more interesting, turn the points on an axis, so the lines point out the *diagonals*.

THE PENTACLE is a five-pointed star. It represents the four elements, with the added "fifth" dimension of spirit and mystery. The five points also represent the human body, with the head, two arms and two legs. It has been used widely as a symbol of magic and transformation, most particularly to ward off evil. But it's also been widely associated with "black magic" and therefore has a sinister history as well. However, in its original form, it represents wholeness and perfection—the unity of matter merged with divine energy.

When you dance five star points, the top point most logically lands at center front. It's a handy shape to use on both regular proscenium stages and when your audience is in a round.

THE SIX-POINTED star, Star of David or Seal of Solomon, is really two triangles: one upright, one inverted. Together these triangles symbolize a unity of male and female energies. The six-pointed star is said to contain an invisible seventh point in the center, representing the unseen world of spirit and unity with the Divine. For a dancer, this pattern also works well when performing in a round.

A Word on the Clock Face

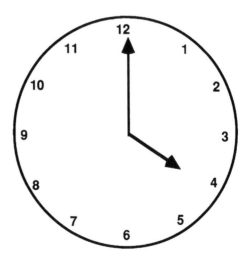

In the next chapter, you will see that I refer to the clock face when determining placement, especially with feet. Within the context of movement and exercise, certain "hours on the clock" help keep alignment precise and diminish risk of injury—and provide an exact positioning we can all understand. The geometry of an old-fashioned clock face is universal and easy (and provides geometry of a secular kind). Pilots use it; so do kindergarten teachers. Picture yourself standing in the center of the clock, with 12 o'clock either directly overhead or in front of you on the floor. Either way, you'll end up in the right position.

Formula Recap

To put it all together in one place, here is a recap of the dance formula and all its components. These represent all the variables that can help you "find your dance" and add infinite modifications. To keep it simple, focus on four shapes and body parts. As you progress, add tempo variations. Finally, to add focus and polish, add directions.

COLUMN A SHAPES	COLUMN B BODY PARTS	COLUMN C CANVAS	COLUMN D TEMPOS	COLUMN E DIRECTIONS
circle figure 8	feet legs	floor walls	slow moderate	line in circle triangle in circle
spiral snake	tailbone, hips spine chest, ribs	ceiling wheel	fast variable	square in circle cross in circle 5-pointed star in circle 6-pointed star in circle
	shoulders, arms			

7 Let's Dance

"The dance is a showing rather than a showing off, a showing of the physical self in the best setting of all, an atmosphere of encouragement and appreciation. It is assumed that all of us, rather than the specially gifted few, are dancers; that everyone can do something, even if it is only two or three movements, and that there is no need for a girl to feel embarrassed or inferior if she is not as skilled as her friends."

—WENDY BUONAVENTURA,
The Serpent of the Nile

"A woman having a good time within her body, sharing her delight in motor expression cannot be exploited."

—JULIE RUSSO MISHKIN AND MARTA SCHILL,
The Complete Belly Dancer

Silly and shallow as this might seem, the right clothes make the dance. It's just not as much fun to celebrate a feminine dance style in baggy sweats, giant T-shirts and big chunky shoes. The spirit of this dance calls for bare feet or dance shoes, flowing fabrics, beaded or jangling hip scarves, clothes that feel sensual against the skin and make rhythms and shapes of their own. Even adding a simple scarf elevates the experience from mere workout to celebration. Hip scarves also make good visual aids for learning hip isolations and veils can be inspired workout tools—much more festive than dumbbells or resistance bands.

Dress the Part

For some of us, the dress-up side of class is the best part. In our casual, unisex, virtual "cross-dressing" society, how often do we really get to adorn, if not *indulge* our femininity in a way that is at once primal and ethereal—even impractical?

Changing from tailored suits, high heels, uniforms and regular "day wear" into "goddess wear" is part of the preparation for the dance. It helps clear the mind, prepare the senses and frame the experience as "special." As we switch from our "everyday selves" into our primordial or higher selves, many of us wonder which is the real self and which is the disguise.

In Defense of "Belly" Dance

Since many but not all of the dance exercises presented here were inspired by belly dance, I'm compelled to run through some fears and misconceptions that surround this dance style. One of the first questions many people ask is "Doesn't belly dance make your stomach fat?" No. Just the opposite. Like any sustained movement, it makes you sweat and burn calories, which makes you *leaner,* which makes the fat around the belly diminish. The movements also address abdominal muscles from more angles than stomach crunches do—so these muscles get stronger but not bigger. When you stick out your belly to do a belly roll (an exercise I haven't included here), it just *looks* larger but it doesn't *make* you fatter. Fatty foods and inactivity do that.

Belly dance is a misnomer since the dance doesn't highlight the belly alone. The term *belly dance* is actually a Western label and is probably a derivative of the Egyptian rhythm called "Baladi." (Many dancers prefer to call it Oriental, Middle Eastern or Egyptian dance.) Whole routines can be built around hip rolls, body waves, shoulders, arms, fingers, head and neck.

The next question is "Well, if it doesn't make you fat, why are so many belly dancers large?" Some belly dancers are large because large belly dancers are often considered more desirable, especially in Arab cultures. Dancers aren't large *because* they belly dance. They're large because of eating habits, genetics, perhaps because they dance very gently and take no other form of exercise. Done for a sustained thirty minutes, even at a slow to moderate pace, belly dance is quite a workout which provides aerobic benefits, strength and flexibility, and burns approximately 300 to 400 calories per hour.

Except in the most progressive places, belly dance seldom appears on the roster at established dance schools or health clubs. Many classical dance schools don't regard it as a legitimate form of dance. Actually, it is one of the most expressive and delicious forms of dance there is. It requires a high level of skill to do well but not such a high level to do and *enjoy*. Many health clubs don't put it on the schedule because they don't see it as a workout. In fact, it's a great workout that you can make as athletic as you want to.

One drawback in some styles of belly dance is the small amount of leg work. So, to create a complete workout I've added a section called "Dancer's Legs." The veil work included here gives a great upper-body workout that benefits back, abdominals, obliques, chest, shoulders and arms, to some degree. But biceps and triceps involvement is minimal; so some supplementary weight work, especially for those muscles, will add strength that the veil does not. (See *A Woman's Book of Strength* for a total list of weight exercises.)

My "dance formula" is not pure belly dance and doesn't pretend to be. (For a complete offering of belly dance styles, videos and costumes, from tribal to cabaret, see *The Middle Eastern Dance Video Sourcebook* in Sources at the end of this book.) However, I hope the presence of simplified belly dance moves makes this dance style more accessible, even lifts the "veil of confusion" that surrounds it. After all, its ancient sensibilities serve timeless yearnings of the spirit and, at the same time, satisfy our modern desires for practical, physical gains.

The Belly Dance–Birth Connection

There is a popular legend that the hip and torso movements of belly dance began as a fertility dance, also as a preparation for childbirth—even as a form of entertainment to distract and soothe women going through labor. But the legends don't necessarily reveal the truth. It makes sense that belly dance would be used as a fertility dance, since it's very sexy—and that's always good for fertility! As a preparation for childbirth, the pelvic movements *can* prepare those muscles used most in childbirth. As for entertainment during childbirth, that one is hard to believe. (Women who've been through childbirth agree that watching a belly dancer during delivery would be the last thing they'd want to do.) Perhaps, if the attendant belly dancers had also been midwives, they could have "danced" the birth mother through waves of pain—and served a useful function. Or perhaps they simply entertained the family awaiting the birth. We really don't know what's true.

What *is* true, however, is that the hip, abdominal and lower back motions of belly dance can help women before, during and especially *after* pregnancy:

• *Before* pregnancy, these moves tone the muscles that will be used the most, especially the deep transverse abdominals.

• During the *first two trimesters* of pregnancy these motions can ease lower-back pain, as long as the movements are gentle and small. They also help a woman retain her sense of beauty and grace as her body gets larger. In the *last trimester*, however, the hips and torso feel practically immobile and any kind of twisting or undulating movement is difficult if not impossible to perform—and thus should be avoided. At this point, gentle shoulder and arm movements (like Exercise #14, "Snake Arms") work best—and can be done either standing, seated or lying on your left side. (Lying on the left side keeps the blood flowing freely to the uterus. Lying on the right or on your back suppresses the blood supply, which could cause premature labor.) Such shoulder-arm movements can actually spread relief down the entire spine. In the *final* stages of pregnancy, it's wise to *forgo full body dancing* and just walk or do yoga or water exercise.

• The hip, belly and torso moves are most beneficial *after* giving birth. During pregnancy and birth the muscles that get most stretched are the *pelvic floor muscles* (the Kegel muscles) and the *transverse abdominals* (deep abdominal muscles that act as a torso "girdle"). Pre- and postnatal exercise specialists will tell you to do at least a hundred Kegel exercises a day during pregnancy and begin again the day after delivery. (Internally squeeze as if stopping the flow of urine. Hold for ten seconds. These should be performed every day throughout a woman's life.) *About three to four weeks after a vaginal* delivery and at least *six weeks after a C-section*, you can begin to "hollow" out the abdominal muscles like a bowl while doing crunches to work transverse abdominals; i.e., pull abdominal muscles *down* to the floor as you lift your head up. Both of these exercises can help you regain and maintain muscular elasticity. (If you don't tone up these muscles in the months after childbirth, you may be in for a lifetime of incontinence and a belly that pooches out.) But the transverse abdominals also get a great workout with the hip and rib cage motions featured here. (See exercises 8, 9, 10, 11, 12 and 13.) To involve transverse abdominals, pull in belly muscles (and allow them to naturally flutter out again) as you move hips and rib cage.

In short, used wisely, "belly dance" moves can be good medicine to help you prepare for pregnancy, ease discomfort during your first two trimesters and most effectively help you recover from giving birth. Of course, if you choose to do this or *any* exercise during pregnancy or after delivery, especially by C-section, get your doctor's permission before you start. Keep in mind, you also don't *have* to give birth to enjoy the muscular benefits imbedded in these motions.

The Busy Woman's Dancing Meditation

I. The Busy Woman's Dancing Meditation

You don't have to formally dance or even stand up to experience the power of feminine dancing. This first exercise is good for a woman on the move and provides a way to tap into the power of the pelvis before rushing off to a busy day. It requires no technique at all—and is the dance form boiled down to its essence. Fidgety types might also find it easier than sitting still to meditate.

Sit on a high, hard pillow or a chair with a pillow on it—or better yet, if you have one, a large ball, like those used in exercise physiology. (Current brand names include: Physioball, Exer-ball, Thera-ball.) It's important that whatever you're sitting on allows you room to rock the pelvis.

Twirl on the tip of your tailbone! Draw any or all of the shapes: circles, figure 8's, spirals and snake. Start with tiny, subtle motions and let all moves originate out of the pelvis. Allow stomach muscles to fully contract and extend as you breathe into the belly. As you become more comfortable with the pelvic rocking, add arm movements to complement your "dance." (Try "Snake Arms," Exercise 14.)

The Dance Begins . . .
Begin with a Blessing: Clear, Breathe and Ground

Before dancing, it helps to clear the mind and prepare the body. Begin by taking notice of the simple things: your body, this opportunity to move, the space you dance in, the music that moves you, the company of each other and the spirit that informs the dance. Then, if time permits, move onto Exercises 2, 3 and 4 for clearing, breathing and "grounding." These help you "come back into your body" if you've been in your head too long and also improve your balance, energy and leg power.

2. Belly Breathing

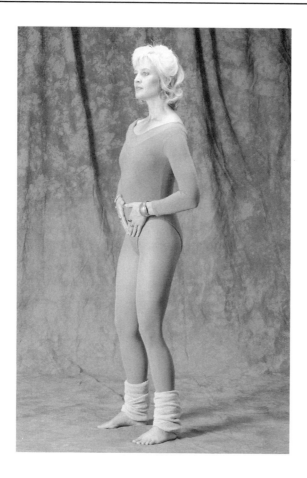

Place your hands on your belly and inhale deeply so it fills like a bellows. Inhale through the nose, not the mouth. The nose was designed as a perfect inhaling device. Nostril hairs filter out impurities and the nasal passages warm the breath. As babies we breathe naturally into the belly. But as we get older, our breathing becomes shallow. We've also been schooled in the importance of holding in the stomach. Here the objective is to stick it out!

To fill the belly with air, first exhale *all* your air out through the mouth, and then push out any excess. Hold the breath out as long as you can. *Then* inhale. That should get air into the belly, like priming a pump. Take at least five full rounds of breath, holding the air all the way in and out as it feels comfortable. Become aware of the spaces between breaths.

Focusing on the breath is very difficult and many of us get confused when we're supposed to differentiate between lungs and diaphragm, nose and mouth. If that's too much for you, just breathe. Breathe through your whole body, in through your pores, up your tailbone, into the pelvis, even up the birth canal!

Open the awareness in your sexual center, the "root chakra." Feel the connection between birth canal/genitals, pelvis, tailbone and the Earth. Tai Chi practitioners are often taught to keep this space between genitals and anus (called the "perineum") closed to prevent energy "leakage." I like to *open* this area because as a woman and a dancer, I feel much more powerful and balanced when I dance with an awareness of this center. It doesn't feel like self-exposure or an energy drain. It feels powerful.

The stance. Stand with feet slightly wider than hip-width apart, toes turned to 11 and 1 o'clock. To find your proper balance, rock forward onto balls of feet then back onto heels. Notice how your entire carriage shifts and certain muscles tense or release when weight is forward or back (that's what happens when posture is bad). Find the center. Your weight should be evenly balanced on the center of each foot, right under your instep.

Try to stack ankles, knees, hips and shoulders, like nesting plates, over the center of each foot. Soften knees and *allow* weight to sink down. (Don't force yourself down. Let it be more like a house settling down over time.) The legs should feel buoyant, springy, ready for action. Your alignment should feel natural, even if the position doesn't (most people feel awkward standing like this at first). But worrying about exact position can be a hindrance. It's more important to relax than get it right.

This stance is based on the "horse stance" from martial arts, as basic to that world as a plié is to dance. The horse stance is a bent-kneed parallel stance used as a "ready" position from which you can punch, kick, block or turn and deflect an attack. When I learned it, however, it felt bowlegged, was tough on the knees and also seemed like a man's creation in that it didn't allow for a woman's wider pelvis. Female thigh bones don't hang straight like a man's but come down on an inward angle (called a "Q angle." This more pronounced angle sometimes causes knee pain when we run). In making this "more feminine," I widened the stance, rotated the hips outward in the sockets, lightly pressed open the knees and shifted the weight back into the hips to open the pelvis.

From here imagine golden chains that extend from the tailbone and the soles of the feet and wrap down into the ground. Legs become as rooted and alive as tree trunks.

(Note: Each exercise contains right- and left-brain instructions to accommodate the different ways we learn. I'd suggest reading both versions to get a full understanding of how the exercise can be done. If an exercise works one side of the body, be sure to repeat the exercise on the other side.)

3. Play with the Golden Ball

Imagine your body is a clear glass vessel, filled with a warm, golden liquid.

Right-brain instructions: Feel the source of that warmth, like a golden sun in your belly. Now, gather a ball of that "light" and hold it in your hands—one hand on top, one below. Start massaging the golden ball as if it were a cloudlike substance, cotton candy, a handful of bubbles. Draw a figure 8 with your arms, as if you were juggling the ball. Let your torso naturally follow the arms (your hips tend to turn toward whichever arm is on top). As your weight shifts from leg to leg, sink your weight *down*.

Left-brain instructions: Draw figure 8's with your arms. Try to keep palms facing each other so you feel the "ball" in your hands. (If you can't feel the "ball" at first, don't worry about it. The point is to relax and let the energy flow.) Turn your hips in the direction of the hand with the palm facing down.

As you loosen up, your hips will begin to draw a figure 8 on the floor, following the arms. Try not to force or will this to happen. Let it flow. When you're done, gather the energy ball back into its original size and let it absorb back into your belly.

4. Simplified Tai Chi Balance Walk P

(Note: from here on in, all exercises marked with a P promote pelvic power!)

The secret to the Tai Chi Walk is shifting weight between each leg and *sinking down* with every step. This movement activates pelvic stabilizing muscles (inner and outer hip) also quadriceps, gluteus and a little bit of hamstring. It feels both very grounding and slightly hypnotic to walk this way. Focus on legs first. Later you can employ the same arm-hand moves you used in "Play with the Golden Ball." When starting, put your primary focus on the weight shifts.

Right-brain instructions: This is basically a forward walk, shifting 100 percent of your weight with every step. As you step out, foot goes forward on a diagonal. Slowly shift all your weight to that forward leg. Sink down, find your balance and bring the back leg in to meet it. Turn your pelvis toward the other leg. Step out. Repeat on other side.

Left-brain instructions: Start with feet hip distance apart and parallel (feet at 12 o'clock).

1. Sink 100 percent of your weight onto your left leg. Turn pelvis and right foot to 2 o'clock. Step out with that foot. Slowly shift 100 percent of your weight onto your right leg and sink down. (Don't let knee extend beyond toes.)

2. Bring your left foot to meet your right foot. Sink down farther. Turn pelvis to the left. Then step out with left to 10 o'clock. Shift weight to that leg. Sink down.

To keep this simple think: "step, shift, sink." If you lose your balance, you need to *sink down more.* Do this slowly enough so you can control each part of the motion. Continue for as long as you want. This step also travels backwards.

Variation: Simply shift weight from leg to leg (and sink down each time) without taking a step.

Dancing the Shapes

The following movements are just some of the many variations you'll find once you start playing with shapes. These are the basics from which you can create a dance.

Be conscious of your body position.

Don't:

- Arch your back in a dangerous position
- Lock knees, elbows, hips or "throw" your shoulders
- Move beyond your sense of muscular control
- Dance so hard that you can't talk for minutes after you stop
- Exacerbate areas where you already have pain

Do:

- Breathe
- Give yourself ample time to warm up and cool down
- Allow torso muscles to be fully involved in the motions so they provide abdominal and back support
- Relax your shoulders as much as possible

You can use these shapes both as a warm-up and in your dance.

In your warm-up:

- Make a shape with just one body part
- Repeat each shape for a minimum of eight times
- Work through the entire body
- Stay in place

As you dance, you will naturally add more layers of complexity:

- Move several body parts at once
- Repeat a step as little or as often as you want
- Add tempo changes, movement punctuations, muscle textures (i.e., soft, hard) and other sorts of "color"
- Move with the shapes through space

You may notice I haven't included many spirals in the following exercises. Spirals work best as you move *through* space—and that's hard to show in a book. You can, however, substitute spirals wherever you might draw circles and figure 8's—especially with hips, ribs and arms.

FEET

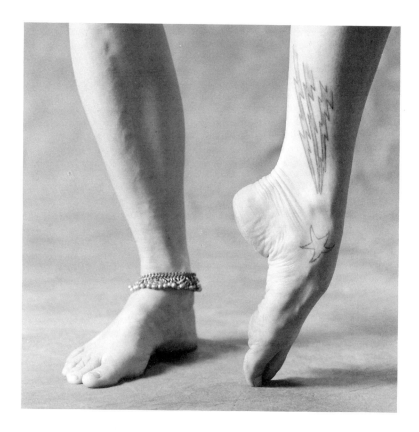

Feet are the unglamorous, unsung heroines of dance. They're often bound inside our shoes but they crave freedom, air between the toes, the full ability to point, flex, scrunch sand or even pick up pencils! Dancers can appreciate the exquisite beauty in a callused, knuckled, working dancer's foot; but to other people, such feet look deformed. Feet are our pads, our paws, our sensing devices.

I prefer to dance barefoot or at least wear dance shoes with a thin sole so I can "feel" the floor. Most aerobic shoes don't let you point or rise up onto your toes very easily because they lack arch flexibility. They were designed for pounding, not dancing. Look for dance shoes or dance *sneakers* if you must wear shoes. If you need the arch and ankle support an aerobic shoe gives you, you might be using too much impact. Let the energy spring from your *torso,* not from bouncing on legs and feet.

The foot is our only concrete connection between the body and the ground (the pelvic connection to the Earth is symbolic and requires a leap in concentration). Upward from the feet, proper alignment is a matter of balance and strength. Without a good "foot connection," alignment can get thrown off. So in honor of the feet, I often begin with some of these classics.

5. Classic Footwork

Stand with feet together. Open toes to 10 and 2 o'clock (ballet's "first position").

• Press onto the ball of one foot, then up to toe point. Lower the ball of the foot, then heel. Keep supporting leg bent. Repeat or alternate.

• Raise both heels to warm up feet and calves but emphasize coming *down* rather than lifting up. This is easier on balance. Afterwards, bend knees, keeping heels on floor (a "demi plié") to relax calves. To work your buttocks even more, pretend you're holding a balloon between your knees as you raise and lower heels. Do this 16 to 32 times without interruption. Stretch afterwards.

• Stand on one leg and circle the other ankle in both directions. Repeat on the other side.

• Tap toes to warm up shins.

• Spread and scrunch toes.

Try to sense the floor as if you had "eyes" on the bottoms of your feet. Foot position also determines the amount of rotation in your hip. To establish your foot-hip connection, try these next two exercises.

BODY PART	SHAPE	DRAW ON THE
feet (ankles)	semicircles	floor

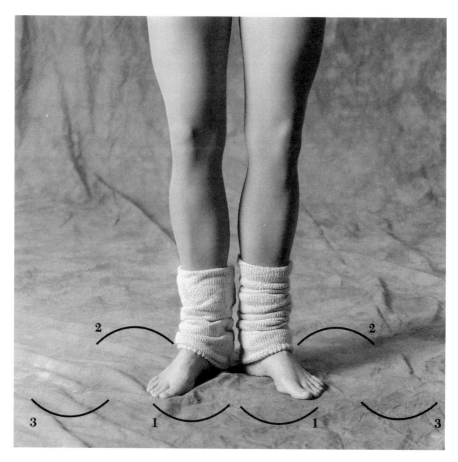

Right-brain instructions: Stand with heels together. Open toes out, then heels out, toes again, heels again, toes one more time—and walk them back in.

Left-brain instructions: Stand with heels together. Simultaneously, take left toes to 10 o'clock, right toes to 2 (ballet's "first position" again). From here, simultaneously open left heel to 8 o'clock, right heel to 4 (a pigeon-toed stance). (Open toes and heels a total of three times and you're in position for the stance in Exercise 2; five times and you're in a solid ballet second position, ready for wide pliés and Exercises 26 and 27).

BODY PART	SHAPE	DRAW ON THE
feet, legs	semicircles	floor

Right-brain instructions: Draw a semicircle on the floor with your toes. Leg moves forward or back, traveling like a compass around the supporting leg. Repeat several times on one leg or alternate legs. As you shift weight from leg to leg, be sure to reestablish your balance (use the same principle as in your rooted Tai Chi Walk). Try moving arms up and over in the opposite direction of the leg for a balanced, whole-brain move. This is a great one to do on the beach, so you can see your semicircles in the sand.

Left-brain instructions: Stand in ballet first position (heels together, toes at 10 and 2 o'clock), knees bent. Slide the right leg straight behind to 6 o'clock and bring it around to the front to 12 o'clock, so your foot draws a semicircle on the floor. Do the same with the other foot. Repeat with same leg or alternate.

HIPS

Since the hips are the source of all powerful movement, they need to be both relaxed and strong. Full, rounded hip movements make you strong and articulate down to the smallest muscles (and they don't hurt your sex life, either!). Tie a scarf around your hips so you can better see your hip motions. If the scarf makes noise, you'll fully involve three senses: feeling, seeing, hearing.

Hip moves, as I mentioned, are good for new moms, as well as for runners, fitness walkers, women who do step aerobics or anyone with *tight* hips. They provide potent medicine for a troubled spirit as well—and are especially good for women who feel battered either physically, emotionally or both. These motions massage the body, soul and self-esteem.

You will probably find that it feels more natural moving in one direction than the other. Be sure to work on the unnatural side, so you don't favor the side you do well (and end up stronger and limping on one side). As you begin with hips, keep upper-body movement minimal. Imagine your chest is lifted and sitting on a shelf so your hips hang free. With all hip movements, work with feet together or hip-distance apart, parallel or turned out, whichever is most comfortable. Keep knees soft and springy but don't bounce up and down. Let heels naturally rise off the floor as they want to. However, work toward keeping both heels *down* to achieve greater hip fluidity. Keeping heels on the floor gives your dance a sense of "earthiness." Raising one or more heels gives your dance a "lift."

BODY PART	SHAPE	DRAW ON THE
Single hip	circles	wall

Right-brain instructions: Begin getting a feel for hip circles by focusing on one hip only. Turn one hip toward the front and draw full circles (not ovals) on the wall in front of you with that hip. As you reverse directions and/or change hips notice which way is more challenging and spend time on that side to loosen up. Pull in abdominals for all-over torso control as hips rotate. Keep shoulders still. Hands look best at hips, shoulder height or higher (or alternate).

Left-brain instructions: As you circle one hip, put more than half your weight on your supporting leg. Hit all the hours of the clock as you rotate. Beware of overarching your back. Remember to keep knees soft.

Variation: Draw small circles, medium circles, big circles, circles inside of circles. Pivot on the ball of your supporting foot and draw a pack of circles that spread from a center point like petals on a flower.

9. Hip Figure 8's #1

P

BODY PART	SHAPE	DRAW ON THE
one or both hips	figure 8	floor

Right-brain instructions: You might find this easier if you focus first on one hip (the other hip will naturally come into play). Draw a figure 8 several times in one direction. Reverse. If one direction is easier than the other, work on the more "difficult" side. As you get comfortable, put focus on both hips. But think "hips only" so you isolate your lower body. Bend knees for more mobility. Arms look best at hips, shoulder height or one up, one down.

Left-brain instructions: Draw your figure 8 this way: a clockwise circle with right hip, followed by a counterclockwise circle with the left. Do this many times before reversing directions. Keep chest and shoulders facing front as hips travel forward and back.

Variation: Try the figure 8 with one big head and one little one, each with different rhythms.

10. Hip Figure 8's #2 *P*

BODY PART	SHAPE	DRAW ON THE
both hips	figure 8	front wall

Right-brain instructions: Draw a figure 8 on the wall with both hips. Begin by taking one hip "down, out to the side, and up." Repeat on the other side. This is a fundamental move in belly dance. Keep knees soft. As your hip drops, allow knee on that same side to bend. You may find certain parts of the motion where you have little control of your hips. Slow down to gain control and loosen tight hips. Arms look best at shoulder height or hands on hips (or one arm up, one down). Or try to synchronize this with Snake Arms (Exercise 14).

Left-brain instructions: Drop your right hip down (and bend your right knee). Then push right hip out to the side and up (so you trace a counter-clockwise circle with that hip). Drop left hip down (and bend left knee). Again, push it out to the side and up (so you trace a clockwise circle). At first, you might need to lift your heels as hips lift to achieve more mobility. Later try keeping heels down for a greater hip stretch.

Variation: Try reversing directions, so your figure 8's travel up, out and down. Or try a figure 8 (in either direction) with a big head on one side, a small one on the other.

11. Snake Hips

BODY PART	SHAPE	DRAW ON THE
both hips	snake	up the wall

Right-brain instructions: Put one foot behind the other and lift your front heel. "Draw" a snaking, wavy motion with hips crawling up and down the wall so that the torso waves in a vertical line (like sea grass). Although the move comes from the hips, the rib cage naturally follows (as if on the end of a whip). Don't think too hard about this. Just relax into the motion and undulate forward and back. This can become a traveling move. Arms look best at shoulder height or above or one up, one down.

Left-brain instructions: With your tailbone, draw a wavy line up the wall. Be sure hips move *forward and back*, not side to side. Bend knees to allow body to rise or sink. If your whole torso wants to wiggle, let it. To get the full abdominal benefit and protect the lower back, pull in abdominal muscles as you lean torso slightly back.

Variation: Mix small undulations with deep, dramatic ones.

Rib Cage

The rib cage is a mostly unsung, uncelebrated part of the body, which has inspired little fantasy or poetry, aside from Adam's rib (not a favorite fable among goddess worshipers). Ribs provide simple armor for heart and lungs. Because there's no great demand for rib cage motion in regular daily activities, most people lack articulation in this part of the body. Consequently many people let their chests sink in and shoulders fall forward (a victim's posture). To add balance to expressive hip motions, rib cage movement is essential in dance—and will improve your posture. Isolating the ribs also calls on deep abdominal muscles, including: the rectus abdominus, obliques and transverse abdominals.

12. Rib Cage Circles #1

BODY PART	SHAPE	DRAW ON THE
rib cage	circles	floor

Right-brain instructions: Before you launch into circles, try hitting four points of a square: front, side, back, side with your sternum (your breast bone). Now round off the edges and rotate rib cage in a circle. Change directions.

Left-brain instructions: As the circle moves back, don't completely collapse in the chest. Keep the contraction small. However, as the circle moves forward, fully *extend* the chest forward. Keep your lower back as still as possible. Hold abdominals in. Move clockwise and reverse.

Variation: Try an angle that's halfway between the floor and the front wall, so the chest reaches both forward and *up.* The 45-degree, upwardly pitched angle adds drama by highlighting the most interesting part of the lift.

13. Rib Cage Circles #2

BODY PART	SHAPE	DRAW ON THE
rib cage	circle	wheel

In this exercise, your motion will be forward, up, back and down.

Right-brain instructions: Put your finger on your breastbone to locate the origin of motion. Draw a circle on the wall, across the ceiling, down the wall and across the floor, like a wheel. Counterclockwise is easier but clockwise is more dramatic because of the emphasized lift in the chest as your torso rolls back. Once you get it, remove your hand from your breastbone and raise one arm so you don't block the view of your chest.

Left-brain instructions: As the chest lifts, stretch abdominals—but control the arch in the lower back. As the chest drops, contract abdominals. This is a great abdominal and lower-back exercise if you control the motion. And it's a lot more fun than crunches and hyperextensions.

Variation: As you become more comfortable with this, allow hips to move naturally in opposition to torso. This is another example of "don't think about it too hard." But when chest lifts forward, hips go back. When chest is back, hips go forward. Adding hips makes this no longer a circle but a body wave, a snake through the torso, similar to Exercise 11—but the origin of the motion is the rib cage, not the hips. Avoid hyper-arching lower back.

SHOULDERS, ARMS

Since most of us walk around with armored shoulders, dance can provide shoulder *relief.* To make your dance beautiful, keep your shoulders relaxed, down and slightly back. You can't raise your arms with grace if your shoulders are tight or lifted. Tight shoulders give movement a robotic look.

Arms complement full body motion and lend the most dramatic shapes and lines. Arms frame the body and the face. Try dancing *only* with arms. There are too many arm variations to mention here. Run through all four shapes, using just shoulders, then add one arm and two. Place those shapes on the floor, the wall, the ceiling. Reverse directions. Hold one arm steady, while the other moves. Here are two favorites that can be varied in many ways.

14. Snake Arms

BODY PART	SHAPE	DRAW ON THE
shoulders, arms	snake	wall

Right-brain instructions: Build up to this. First lift one elbow. As you lower that arm, lift the other elbow. Now add your wrist to the motion. Finally add the fingers. Imagine you're flicking water off your fingertips and your arms have no bones.

Left-brain instructions: Try getting into it this way: Draw a clockwise circle with right shoulder, counterclockwise with left. As right shoulder moves to the side, lift elbow, so it points up and back. Repeat on left. Gradually add wrists and fingers. As soon as the right arm is lifted and begins to lower, pull up the left arm. One arm is always up, the other down, so they work in opposition.

Variations: Try this with arms parallel to floor, angled 45 degrees over head or one arm higher than the other. Try it with one arm in front and the other to the side.

15. Flamenco Arms

BODY PART	SHAPE	DRAW ON THE
shoulders, arms	figure 8	wall

Right-brain instructions: Flamenco arms are passionate and elegantly frame the body. They switch from dramatically slow or held poses to lightning-fast movement. Draw a figure 8 on the wall in front of you with one arm higher than the other. Imagine you are in a bullfight, lifting the cape for the bull. Keep the same fluidity in arms as in the last exercise— although, if you want to add a Flamenco flourish, flick your wrists and fingers and hold a pose to complete the move.

Left-brain instructions: Circle both arms counterclockwise to the right, clockwise to the left. Reverse.

Variations: Try this with just one arm. Hold the other one still.

WRISTS, FINGERS

Beautiful hands complete your dance. Clumsy hands destroy it. Bring life to every finger and the palm of your hand, and cultivate fluidity in your wrists. Notice the texture of your fingers. Are they rigid, soft? Do they move independently of one another or in a group? Play with every conceivable hand position: try circles, figure 8's, snakes and spirals on the floor, the ceiling, the walls. Lead with thumbs, pinkies, all the different fingers. Try dancing only with your hands. Make your hands swim, wave, caress, weave, stir, pray, receive, push, pull. This is good therapy for preventing (and possibly easing) both carpal tunnel syndrome and arthritis, especially if you work at a computer keyboard all day. If Indian temple dancers could come up with five hundred hand movements, you could probably think of at least five. To emphasize the beauty of your hands, try decorating them with rings, bracelets and a manicure.

16. Hand Dancing

BODY PART	SHAPE	DRAW ON THE
wrists, fingers	all the shapes	floor, walls, ceiling

Right-brain instructions: Bend and rotate your wrists in various positions, keeping movements fluid. Try to use each finger as if you were playing an instrument. Your fingers already make natural shapes when you bend your wrists. Take these shapes and enhance them.

Left-brain instructions: For wrist circles—lead with thumb in one direction, pinkie in the other. For snaking moves—push with the heel of the hand, the "ball" and then fingers.

Variation: Once your fingers can tell whole stories, just for fun, make a fist and dance around. See how expressive you can be with those hands. Dancing without fingers is like speaking without a voice.

Now You're Dancing

The warm-up seamlessly segues into dance. As you make shapes with certain body parts, allow other parts to join in and you're dancing! When you're warm and the music is good, let yourself move.

In class, once I run through the warm-up shapes, I have everyone turn away from the mirror and call out body parts and shapes (for example: "hips, figure 8, wall"). This gives everyone the opportunity to take the shapes they just saw in the mirror and "pattern" them on their own bodies. Improvisation is encouraged. But the rules are these:

- Be conscious of your placement so you don't hurt yourself.

- Don't bump into anybody or invade her space.

- Don't watch or try to copy anyone else.

- If you feel awkward, close your eyes, stop and do one simple move. Then build on it.

Fun Sequence Number One

This mini "routine" gives you an idea of how to string moves together. If you want to make this into a dance instead of an exercise, take out the even two, four and eight counts, so it doesn't look so syncopated and choreographed. For dramatic flair, add tempo variations and mix up bigger movements with small. Work toward making transitions between different movements natural, so your dancing doesn't look choppy. Let it flow.

[Face front]

1. Begin with expressive hands

2. Move into snake arms   4x

[Turn body to diagonal so "audience" can see your 3/4 profile]

3. Pose in Flamenco arms, then continue figure 8 movement   4x

4. Rib circles on floor, one hand up, one on hip   4x

[Face front]

5. Single hip circle, on wall, 2 to the right, 2 to the left,
   arms as above   2x

6. Double hip figure 8's, on the wall, hands on hips   8x

[Turn body to diagonal, so "audience" sees your 3/4 profile]

7. Rib circles, wheel, 1 hand on hip, 1 arm shoulder height   2x

[Add hips into motion, so it segues into next move]

8. Snaking hips, up the wall   4x

[Turn and face the front]

9. Hip figure 8's on the floor   4x

10. Feet-hip semicircles on floor, walking forward (Exercise 7)   4x

[Stop. End in pose. Repeat whole sequence.]

The Veil

Since the myth of Ishtar, the veil has always been a dancer's tool. It flows, it dances and it enhances the dancer's body more for what it suggests than what it displays. The veil is a potent symbol of what is hidden and what can be revealed; it is the thin curtain between innocence and seduction, the holy and indecent, even the world of matter and spirit. The veil also implies the realm that exists *beyond* the obvious. Whoever lifts the veil has the power to reveal what can be seen and by whom. Whoever drapes the veil (or enforces it) has the power to determine what must be held secret and why. The veil isn't a mask as much as a gauzy cover on the truth. Yet it has the power to heighten our mystery and draw others to us for the secrets we seem to contain.

In Islamic countries, the veil was enforced upon women as a way to protect *men* from their desire—not to protect women from men. The thick veil worn by many Islamic women renders the body sexless by hiding all feminine characteristics, even the face. Many Islamic women who once rejected this sort of veil as a symbol of repression have since reembraced it as a form of protection. It lets them pass through the world without interruption or the invasive eyes of men and therefore carries in its sexless drapery a freedom of its own.

The dancer's veil, on the other hand, is usually sheer and clinging, an extension of the body. It moves as we move. With it, however, we also determine what to cover and what to reveal. When Ishtar danced her Dance of the Seven Veils, she did not take off her veils willingly. They were symbols of her power. For that reason, they were not mere accessories but potently charged bargaining chips for the life of her lover. Only by surrendering this power was she able to win. Anything less valuable would not have pleased the "hairy goddess of death."

Sometimes, like Ishtar, we get what we want when we strip off our veils and are willing to be naked and speak the truth. But this isn't always wise, especially out in the world where our powers aren't often acknowledged. It's a good idea, then, to keep a veil handy, at least a metaphorical one to wear when the situation begs us not to reveal everything we know or possess.

It's also a good idea to keep a real veil handy since, aside from being a potent symbol, it's a useful tool. It's a delicious dance partner, a hip sash, a hair tie, a shawl, a one-shouldered drape (especially useful for nursing moms), a skirt, a halter top, a headpiece.

As a dance partner (and exercise tool), veil work is shape making with whipped-cream icing and sugar on the top. It's beautiful, incredibly fun and also quite a workout for torso and arms. Focusing on the veil takes the focus off the self and in the process lessens inhibition and frees movement. The veil tells you by landing on your head or falling on the floor if you haven't quite got the move right. But when you've mastered the movement, the veil flies. Veil dancing, by nature, is vigorous. To keep it moving, you've got to use speed. So use your center and don't be afraid to make that veil soar!

The best-moving materials are silk and chiffon, but anything that flows will do. The heavier the material, the harder it is. You'll feel a big difference between a sheer chiffon, for instance, and an opaque heavier material. Also, if the material has heavy metallic threads in it or beads or embroidery, it might not be weighted evenly and so might be hard to work with. Keep that in mind and use a veil of an appropriate size and weight.

If you haven't been working out, you might want to start with a smaller scarf, about one yard square, and progress up to a bigger size and heavier weight. Everyday veils are easy to make. Buy two to three yards of forty-five-inch-wide material and hem the ends. Fancier veils, like the kinds used by cabaret-style belly dancers, can cost between $25 and $100 or more. (For a list of fancy veil and costume makers, see *The Middle Eastern Video Sourcebook* in Sources.)

To hold your veil, spread out your arms and grasp the edges in your fingertips. If your veil is small, hold the corners. With each exercise be sure to keep your back in natural alignment (don't slump or arch) and work within your "comfort zone." Learn each move standing in place. As you become adept, travel across the floor with it.

Right-brain instructions: Draw a figure 8 with your veil on the wall in front of you. Arms come from the outside in *toward* the center, across the body's midline. The veil trails under each arm, like wings or long, draping sleeves.

Left-brain instructions: Fully extend the top arm as you raise the veil. Arms pivot around the shoulder joint (if this feels uncomfortable, bend your elbow to make the move smaller). Right arm moves in a counter-clockwise direction; left is clockwise. Take each arm slightly *behind* the body before lifting to the front.

Works: Back, chest, shoulders, torso.

18. The Flying Skirt. One-Arm Figure 8's

Right-brain instructions: Anchor one hand on your hip (holding your "skirt"). Let the other hand trace a figure 8 on the wall. Use your elbow, not your shoulder, as the main pivoting joint. This only works in one direction—first out, then in. You'll figure it out soon enough. Imagine you're a Flamenco dancer and the veil is your skirt. Snap it. Have a little attitude!

Left-brain instructions: Bunch the veil in your left hand and hold it on the left hip. Trace a figure 8 on the wall with your right hand. Keep the upper part of your right arm next to your torso. The figure 8 moves counterclockwise on the right circle, clockwise on the left (and the opposite when your left hand works). The veil dances in the space between your knees and over your head.

Works: Shoulders, arms. This is a good resting or transition step between more vigorous veil moves.

19. The Funnel. Circles on the Wall and on the Ceiling

Right-brain instructions: You'll find out right away that before you can continuously circle the veil, you have to flip it behind you and to the side, at the bottom of the turn. Otherwise the veil lands on your head. This "flip" happens in the wrists, elbows and shoulders. It's really a small, figure-8 turn—on the right side if you're moving clockwise. Before you think about it too hard, simply try putting your attention on drawing many circles in the same direction—and the flip movement might take care of itself. Let one arm lead and the other follow in opposition, as if you were holding a big steering wheel (in other words, at the fullest part of the circle, arms are as wide apart as they can be). To make this more vigorous and dramatic, draw the circle on the ceiling (imagine the veil is drawing a funnel). This uses more torso muscles, especially if you create a *full* circle overhead. Hold in abdominals to maintain your "center." If you still don't get this, read the left-brain instructions.

Left-brain instructions: To draw a clockwise circle, start with both arms hanging straight down. Take the right arm slightly *behind* the body on the *right*. This little swishing figure 8 builds momentum. Next, cross right arm over left and bring it up the clock face, in front of your body from about 9 to 12 o'clock. At this point, the left will follow (about "six hours" behind). Don't forget to change directions.

Works: Torso (a great one for abdominals, obliques), back, chest, shoulders, arms.

20. Flapping the Veil. Snaking Move with Both Arms

Right-brain instructions: This one's like waving sand out of a beach blanket. The veil undulates and snakes. Wave the veil either at waist height (easy) or all the way up beyond shoulders (vigorous). Maintain a strong back position. Hold in abdominals. Don't break at the waist.

Left-brain instructions: Start with hands down to the floor (6 o'clock). Lift hands and arms to 3 o'clock (easy, but veil will go higher) or lift all the way to 12 o'clock and back down (harder).

Works: Shoulders, arms.

21. Spiral Turns

Right-brain instructions: Spinning with a veil offers more drama than workout. But it's fun. Take the veil behind you, holding arms wide. Spin with it so it flies behind you (raising one arm higher in the direction of your spin shows more veil). Focus on a spot so you don't get dizzy. You can spin in place or spiral across the floor. It's easiest on your equilibrium if you begin with just one spin at a time. Do any of the above moves between spins. Work up to two and three spins before spinning yourself silly. When you get good at this, try taking the veil higher overhead as you turn!

Left-brain instructions: The left brain has a hard time comprehending spins, so we'll keep it simple. Hold the veil behind you with arms spread wide, parallel to floor or higher. Pivot around your left foot. Right foot travels on ball of foot (called a paddle turn).

Works: Your sense of balance and focus, your dramatic flair! To transition out of a spin and stop the world from turning, try a few Funnels or Flap the veil.

Fun Sequence Number Two—With the Veil

Again, this routine is geared for practice, not performance. To perform with a veil, simply do fewer repetitions of each exercise, and vary your tempos and the size of your movements as the music dictates.

Wings, start on right	8x
Flying Skirt, work right side	8x
Funnel, overhead, clockwise	8x
Flap	8x
Flying Skirt, work left side	8x
Funnel overhead, counterclockwise	8x
[Keep veil behind you on last funnel]	
Spiral Turn, counterclockwise	2x
[Bring veil to front with left arm overhead, as in a funnel turn]	
Flap	8x
Spiral Turn, clockwise	2x
Flap	8x
Repeat from the top	

Dancer's Legs

These leg exercises come from ballet, jazz, modern dance, martial arts and bodybuilding. They add strength, coordination, balance and grace and work either as a warm-up, workout or cool down. You'll work your legs harder when they are "fresh." If these exercises leave your legs feeling too heavy to dance, do them afterwards.

The balance pole featured here serves many purposes: it's a portable ballet barre as well as a visual aid for alignment, and it helps with upper-body stretches as well. The pole shown here is a cane with a rubber tip. (You can also use a standard 4-foot "closet dowel," available in most hardware stores for around $2.50. Put 1 1/4-inch rubber furniture bumpers on both ends to prevent skids and scratches on a wooden floor.) Use a light grip on the pole so you don't become overly dependent on it.

To find your optimal balancing stance, soften the knee of your supporting leg and sink weight down (as in the Tai Chi Balance Walk) before beginning the exercise. Complete the exercise with *both* legs before doing the next exercise so your supporting leg doesn't poop out.

22. Outer/Inner Thigh Cross and Lift   *P*

Right-brain instructions: Reach your right leg directly out to the side (keep toes facing forward to keep leg "in parallel"; i.e., don't rotate leg open in the hip socket). Then cross that same leg over the body's midline and lift to the other side. *Now* turn out the working leg at the hip, bend knee and flex foot. Keep hips and torso still as you do this.

Left-brain instructions: Imagine you're standing inside a clock face, facing 12 o'clock. Reach right leg to 3 o'clock, no more than 6 to 8 inches off the floor. From there, swing leg across the body to the other side, to 10 o'clock. Lift leg 12 inches off the floor in this position and flex foot and knee.

Works: Hip stabilizers (outer and inner thigh). Good for balance and strength. Do 8 to 20 times and repeat on other side. Work slowly enough that you work with *muscle*, not momentum.

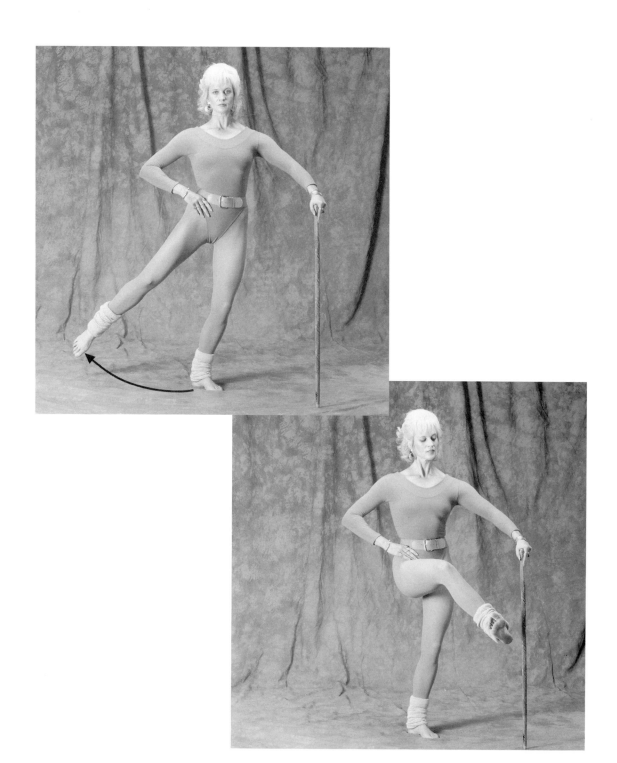

Right-brain instructions: With your right knee, draw a figure 8 on the wall in front of you. As the working leg crosses the body, draw a clockwise circle with your knee. As it opens, draw a counterclockwise circle. Focus on increasing mobility in the hip joint.

Left-brain instructions: Be sure to balance on your supporting leg. Bend the knee and sweep your working leg across your body's midline. Inner thigh of that leg faces in. To complete the figure 8, open the inner thigh so it faces away from you. Lower knee on your working leg and sweep leg to other side. Keep the motion continuous.

Works: Hip stabilizers and some gluteus. Do 8 to 20 times. Repeat other side.

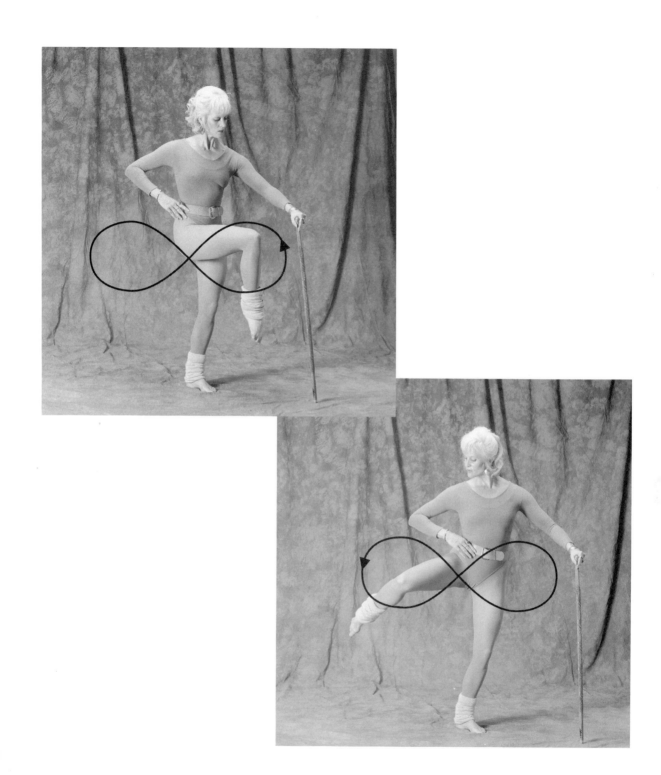

Right-brain instructions: It's a little easier to maintain balance if you push your pole forward on an angle for counterweight. Lean torso slightly forward but keep your chest up and out and abdominals in to maintain good posture. This also gives your leg more range of motion. Press the working leg back, keeping shin parallel to the floor. (Imagine you are trying to make footprints on the wall behind you.) Keep shin of working leg parallel to the floor to avoid using lower back.

Left-brain instructions: Sink weight into your supporting leg, keeping that knee bent for balance. Extend working leg behind you, pushing the sole of the foot toward the wall behind you. But don't straighten leg completely or swing leg with no control. Be sure to keep torso still as leg extends. If this is uncomfortable in your lower back or you feel a limited range of motion, incline torso forward a bit more, to approximately 30 to 45 degrees.

Works: Hamstrings and buttocks. Do this 8 to 20 times each leg. Switch sides. Vary this by keeping working leg turned out or in parallel. To make this more challenging, try adding a light ankle weight, 1 to 5 pounds.

25. Ballet Hamstring Curl

P

Right-brain instructions: In the same position as above, extend one leg behind you. Bend the knee so your foot draws a semicircle in the air. But don't just lift the foot; resist lifting it, as if you were moving through water so you work the muscle in the back of your thigh. Your hamstring is your leg's bicep. Imagine you were flexing and showing it off, as you might show off your arm bicep. To better isolate the hamstrings, lift rib cage, lengthen muscles on front of hip (hip flexors) and squeeze buttocks. Also, hold upper part of working leg still—or you diminish the effectiveness of the exercise by bringing in an extra joint and more muscles than you need to use.

Left-brain instructions: With working leg extended behind supporting leg, lift foot from a 7 to 10 o'clock position. Try this with a pointed foot to make it harder. Flex foot as hamstrings become fatigued. Be sure to hold upper leg still throughout this exercise. Bend the knee only. Swinging the leg adds the hip joint and robs the hamstring of its work.

Works: Hamstrings and torso stabilizers. Do this 8 to 20 times; switch legs. This also works well with a light ankle weight, from 1 to 5 pounds.

Pliés

Some notes on the plié. These next two exercises combine the pliés of ballet (for inner thigh, quadriceps, buttocks strength and shape), the squats and lunges of bodybuilding (for *more* strength and shape), with the deep, held stretches and isometrics of martial arts (for grit, endurance and flexibility). Done in the deepest positions, these are advanced exercises. Beginners should lower only halfway down or as far as bearable. (These aren't easy or comfortable at first. But as you get used to them, your tolerance will increase.)

The secret of success here is in moving *slowly*, holding the deepest stretches and contractions for at least two seconds each. Pliés appear simple (you bend and straighten your knees—what's hard about that?). But it took me years before I understood how to do them effectively. Pliés begin in the *hips,* not in the knees. In other words, before the knees bend, you should feel a release in the hip sockets. Hips actually lift *up* before lowering down. Think of your hips as two gears that control all the movement.

Also imagine that your legs don't just end at the pelvis—but in the armpits. (Every time you straighten your legs, imagine that you're pulling up a pair of support hose all the way to your chest). Pliés are full of oppositions. As you lower the torso pull *up* through the spine and head and keep heels down. As you lift the torso, press legs and shoulders *down*. Relax and stretch as you lower. Work as you lift up again.

Your wide plié stance should be two to three times wider than your hips, with knees directly over ankles or feet—but not extending beyond toes. To get here, stand with heels and toes together and open toes, heels, etc., five times (as I mentioned in Exercise 5). As you bend your knees, keep buttocks tucked *under* shoulders (taking buttocks *behind* hips is a squat). Lower pelvis so knees bend at forty-five- to ninety-degree angles.

I'm often asked, "What's the difference between a plié and a squat?" and "What is each one good for?" In short, both make you strong. The squat works well for lifting extra weight because the hips, lower back and knees are in a stable position, with feet parallel or slightly turned out. I usually recommend squatting while holding dumbbells instead of a bar across the neck (which compresses the vertebrae). However, in class, I seldom bother with squats (unless they're superslow and deep) because without weight they don't do *enough*, at least for me. In class, I prefer the plié because it feels more graceful, comfortable and challenging and provides a better stretch. Also, as I get older, I rely less on weighted leg work with free weights and machines and rely more on "naked," unweighted deep pliés and lunges to keep my legs strong.

As for specific differences between the two, here goes:

Wide Second-Position Pliés	Squats
Legs are approximately *2 to 3* times wider than hips.	Legs are *1 to 2* times wider than hips.
Open toes, heels, *5 times.*	Open toes, heels *3 times.*
Feet are turned to *10 and 2* o'clock.	Feet are turned to *11 and 1* o'clock.
Hips stay *under* shoulders.	Hips *sit back* behind shoulders.
Torso stays *upright.*	Torso *inclines* slightly forward.
Legs *rotate* out in hip socket.	Legs are *parallel* or slightly rotated.
Best performed *without weight*, for knees and back.	Knees and back can handle *extra weight.*
Targets buttocks, quads, inner thigh.	Targets buttocks, quads, inner thigh.

One final word on pliés: External rotation or turning out from the hip is held as a high-and-mighty example of prowess in ballet. But excessive turn out is bad for the knees and causes instability in the hip. A slight turn out is all that's necessary, with feet at 10 and 2 o'clock (not 9 and 3!). However, when legs straighten, imagine that hips rotate outward even more, even though feet stay put. This adds a mental twist to an otherwise straight up-and-down motion (like adding coil to a spring). It ultimately adds power.

26. Power Pliés   P

A right- and left-brain mix.

1. Stand in a wide ballet second position. Slowly bend knees to a 45- to 90-degree angle.

2. Keeping chest forward and abdominals held in, incline torso 45 to 90 degrees forward (your ideal position is parallel to the floor, but work up to it). Place hands inside knees to stretch them open. Take your time. If you do this to music, use 4 slow beats to rock forward.

3. Return torso to upright position, but keep knees bent (stay down). Make sure buttocks return to just under the shoulders. This is the moment of truth: *pause* for a moment down in plié to allow legs to sink into a deeper stretch. Again, take 4 beats to return to upright plié. If you really want to make this challenging, stay down longer.

4. Slowly return to standing position and begin again. As you straighten legs, imagine you're squeezing a giant balloon between your thighs. Take another slow 4 counts to come up. Repeat series at least twice. This one's a zinger, and slower is harder.

Right-brain instructions: Go into a demi plié (half plié). Draw a clockwise circle on the wall with hips. The stronger you are, the deeper you can go—and the stronger you'll get. Make sure knees don't extend beyond toes as hips travel to the side. Keep hips directly under shoulders. Reverse directions.

Left-brain instructions: Hips travel only about 4 to 5 inches to either side, so the entire circle should only be 8 to 10 inches in diameter. Hipbones can either stay parallel to the floor or, for variation, raise one hip in the direction you're moving (i.e., lift right hip when you move to right, lift left when hips travel left).

Works: Buttocks, quadriceps, inner thigh. Be sure to work in both directions. Alternate or do up to 8 times in the same direction (more than that is supertough!).

Right-brain instructions: Take a long stance, as in a fully extended cross-country ski position. Hold pole for balance. Be sure back heel is up and both knees are slightly bent. Incline torso slightly forward to focus work in the buttocks, as opposed to the thighs. Keep chest out. Bend front knee so that thigh is parallel to the floor. As you straighten front leg, press into your front *heel* (to target buttocks even more). Most of the work happens in the front leg. Back knee stays resilient and bends when it needs to.

Left-brain instructions: Take a hip-distance, parallel stance. Slide one leg back to get into position. If right foot is forward, hold pole in left. Incline torso 20 to 45 degrees. As you bend front knee, keep it over *ankle*, not toes. As you straighten the leg, press into your *heel*. Torso stays inclined throughout. To add intensity and more buttocks work, try this with front foot elevated about 6 to 8 inches. Buttocks can drop *below* the knee if elevated, as long as knee stays over or *behind* the ankle.

Works: Quadriceps, buttocks, some hamstring and inner thigh.

Stretching with the Pole

These three exercises are but a few "pole stretches." All target muscles that get worked in dance. In the last two exercises, the pole "lends architecture" to the stretches. In other words, the pole keeps you in the right position and therefore helps you safely stretch farther. These stretches (along with optional floor stretches) are a nice way to end a workout.

29. Lower Back Stretch

Using the pole for balance, open legs to hip-distance stance or wider (feet can be slightly turned out). Bend knees and sit hips back *away* from the pole. Draw clockwise and counterclockwise circles on the wall behind you with your tailbone and/or wag tailbone from side to side in a semicircle. Keep shoulders relaxed as you do this.

30. Side Hip Stretch

Stand in a parallel stance. Hold pole in both hands across your thighs. Sink weight down into right leg (knee is bent) and then lean into right hip. Slide right tip of pole up the right side of your body. Fully extend the right arm so the pole tip reaches to the ceiling or beyond—and look up at the tip. This stretches the entire right side. Hold for at least 10 seconds. Exhale to stretch farther. Repeat on left.

Begin in a ballet first position (heels touching, toes to 10 and 2 o'clock). Slide right leg back behind the body, so that right heel is down and in the 7 o'clock position. Right leg is straight. Left knee is bent. Push pole overhead and slightly to the left of center to stretch your entire right side. Repeat on the other side.

For Instructors and Self-Motivators—Sample Workouts

The four shapes, veil work, leg exercises and pole stretches work together as a whole unit or as modules to plug in to separate or shorter workouts. For instance, the four shapes could serve as a warm-up or a whole workout. The veil work could provide the most vigorous part of a dance workout. The dancer's leg section serves as a lower-body strength and sculpting workout, and the pole stretches could be used as a cool down or added to an entire stretch or yoga workout.

I myself "plug and play" these concepts into different sorts of workouts and classes. Here are three sample workouts.

Dance-Movement Workout: 45 Minutes

Belly breathing, Golden Ball, Tai Chi Walk	5 minutes
Warm-up shapes, isolating body parts	10 minutes
Dancing the shapes (improv, away from mirror)	15 minutes
Veil work	10 minutes
Cool down and pole stretches	5 minutes

Soft-Hard Workout: Dance, Strength and Stretch: 60 Minutes

Warm-up shapes, isolating body parts	10 minutes
Dancing the shapes	15 minutes
Veil work	10 minutes
Upper-body strength, using dumbbells or bands	10 minutes
Dancer's legs, shorter version (fewer exercises or reps)	10 minutes
Pole and floor stretches	5 minutes

Lower-Body Strength and Stretching Workout: 30 Minutes

Belly breathing, Golden Ball, Tai Chi Walk	5 minutes

Dancer's Leg Series, extended version (more reps)
   Outer-inner thigh cross and lift
   Leg figure 8's
   Kickback for Hamstrings and Buttocks
   Ballet Hamstring Curl
   Power Pliés
   Plié Hip Circles
   "Naked Lunges"
	20 minutes

Pole Stretches	5 minutes

Workout Schedule

Since everyone's schedule, capacity and tastes are different it's virtually impossible to give a schedule that works for all. However, how much you do and how often you do it depend on what you want to achieve. To become a better dancer, you should dance at least once—preferably twice—a week and stretch afterwards to maintain flexibility. Add one or two weight workouts a week (for upper and lower body) and see what that leaves time for. Additional yoga stretching, additional cardio workouts? Your body will tell you what it wants and needs. If your dance is very moderate, you may want some additional aerobics. If your dance is highly aerobic, you may not need them.

As for scheduling, in a perfect world, a world without overwhelming responsibilities, an average workout schedule might go like this:

Monday	Dance and stretch
Tuesday	Upper-body workout and stretch
Wednesday	"Power" walk or swim, etc.
Thursday	Dance
Friday	Active rest—yoga
Saturday	Lower-body workout
Sunday	A nice, long, slow hike . . . so you can be ready to dance on Monday!

And When the Dance Is Done . . .

"Performance art is a return to tribal, ritual forms, an exploration of women's mythologies and lost histories."

—ELINOR GADON, *The Once and Future Goddess*

"Into the body, harmoniously developed and carried to its highest degree of energy, enters the spirit of the dance."

—ISADORA DUNCAN

When the dance is done, we thank the forces that move us, unknot our hip scarves, fold up our actual veils and put on our metaphorical ones as we slip back into our worldly disguises: jeans, suits or sweats and retrieve our cars, children, groceries, messages and "real world" personalities. We go home to our families and prepare for the next day of work, errands and tightly packed schedules. Yet we walk out lighter than when we arrived. We are opened, calm, nourished. The glow will last for a day or two but will need tending again soon. Our bodies now yearn for motion that only dance will satisfy. Yet even in stillness, behind a veil no one else can see, there is a part of us inside that is always dancing.

PART THREE

Mind and Future

8   Dancing Through the World

There is no beauty more profound (and perhaps less appreciated) than that of a mature woman who, despite wrinkles, adversities and resistance at every turn, seems to glide above other struggling mortals, in full command of her magic. The spotlight may shine on curvaceous young starlets. But the woman who cultivates a sacred grace has an enduring, luminous sort of elegance, especially when she balances her spirit with a physical practice that brings her pleasure, discipline and mastery. Such a woman seems driven not by a fear of age, decay and death but a desire to make herself and her life into a work of art. She takes her history, her sensibilities, presence, faith, pains and hopes for the future and creates an always-changing, living sculpture. She becomes a World Dancer.

The World Dancer

The World Dancer represents the last phase in a journey toward knowledge. In the Tarot deck, she is the last card in the "major Arcana," twenty-two named cards which signify a journey toward wisdom. The journey begins with the Fool (the one who is aware he knows nothing), stepping off into the void of the unknown, seeking wisdom through adventure. After many transmutations, this traveler returns as a dancer through the ring of experience, with the lights of knowledge in her hands, signifying completion, fruition, understanding. She embodies contradiction, seems ethereal yet earthy, womanly yet androgynous, naked but veiled, young yet old, erotic but imbued with pure spirit, a balance of forces: dark, light, sacred, secular, female and male. She is all things at once, an example of realized potential yet full of potential yet to be explored. Her veil is a symbol of all she knows yet keeps hidden from view—and all things that remain hidden from her. She plants one foot on the ground and lifts the other in the air as if to show she is comfortable dancing in all realms: in the air, on the Earth, in her spirit-body-mind. She contains, as Rachel Pollock says in *Seventy-Eight Degrees of Wisdom, A Book of Tarot,* "rapture beyond words." She is "the unconscious known consciously, the outer self unified with the forces of life, knowledge that is not knowledge at all but a constant ecstatic dance of being."[1]

The World Dancer's journey takes her into the Underworld and gloriously out again. Hers is the passage of a woman who plumbs her depths and returns to herself, complete, satisfied, more powerful, passionate and wiser than if she'd never taken the adventure at all. The World Dancer is the role model for those of us who have opened to the unknown, the unexplored or the forgotten in ourselves, and have even let certain parts of ourselves die so others can be reborn. We have discovered that if we dare to dig deep in ourselves for buried treasure and are willing to excavate with our whole bodies, spirits and intention, regardless of how dirty we get or what others may think, we *become* the treasure. We come out dancing.

The World Dancer's journey inspires us to find what fulfills us even when the world around us discourages such inner adventure, especially when it goes against the prepackaged notions of what health, happiness, love, success and beauty are supposed to be. Her wisdom is the reward for those of us who take the time to celebrate the dark, chaos, confusion, spontaneity and the unknown. She encourages us not to follow the herd but to find the source of *our* power, our voices and the dances that move us. The World Dancer is a role model for thinking, feeling, adventurous women because she has not only embraced her mystery, she weaves it into her dance through life. Without tying her soul and her actions to a source of magic greater than her own, she would not be as fulfilled or fascinating and her dances would spring from a hollow core.

[1]Rachel Pollock, *Seventy-Eight Degrees of Wisdom, A Book of Tarot,* Part 1: The Major Arcana (LondonSan Francisco: Thorsons, Harper Collins, 1980), 124.

"In a temporal
sense, the 'cosmic
dancer' is the essen-
tial self who takes
form again and
again through rein-
carnation of the
soul in different
bodies during vari-
ous lifetimes."

—VICKI NOBLE,
*Motherpeace, A Way
to the Goddess
through Art, Myth
and the Tarot*

"When a woman
can find the
courage to be lim-
ited and to realize
that she is enough
exactly the way she
is, then she discov-
ers one of the true
treasures of the
heroine's journey . . .
She becomes real,
open, vulnerable
and receptive to a
true spiritual awak-
ening."

—MAUREEN
MURDOCK,
The Heroine's Journey

For most women, the journey into our sacred power, into our personal connection to a divinely inspired feminine wisdom, *had* to begin in the body because in order to really learn this lesson, we had to *feel* it course through our flesh, nerves, fascia and bones. We couldn't just read or hear about it. We had to dance with it, breathe it, sing it, smell it, touch it, taste it, give birth to it, get close to the soil so we could hear and feel its pulse beating in sync with our own. Once we have done this, we see the entire world around us as charged with divine potential and therefore we recog-nize the divinity within ourselves. All our actions, then, either reflect this divinity or defy it. All long-term abuses of the body-spirit-mind whether through drugs and alcohol, extremes with food, obsessive exercise routines, total inactivity, harmful relationships, chronically sour moods or even just negative chatter about ourselves or others have no rightful place in our lives. In fact these things border on sacrilege because they cannot support us in being who we really are. They are masks that we ourselves can't see behind.

More of us *are* following the path of the World Dancer. We're beginning to care less, en masse, about the hardness of our buttocks and more about the richness in our hearts. We're dancing (hiking, playing sports, etc.) for different reasons—not as penance but as nourishment. The World Dancer shows us that we don't need to set out on this journey with a clear destina-tion in mind. Sometimes it's best to jump in, like the Fool, without being attached to any particular outcome. Nor do we always need to follow the straightest route to get to a destination. It's usually more fun to enjoy the unfolding, follow the curves, twists and meanders on the path and appre-ciate the riches that are revealed to us. The World Dancer comes into our lives as if to pose the questions: If we don't celebrate ourselves, when will we be celebrated? If we don't dance our dances, when will they ever be danced? If we don't think we're beautiful, who will?

So how can we keep dancing in a world that doesn't necessarily approve of us, agree with our point of view, welcome us without criticism or recog-nize our worth? How can we also let it be known that we no longer sub-scribe only to a stern Father God but welcome the loving, accepting spirit of the Mother—and, in fact, want to *embody* Her, or at least an aspect of Her? How can we "come out" about the Goddess when the majority still regard the concept of feminine divine power (especially when it is cele-brated by circles of women, dancing, singing, howling or otherwise) as pagan, subversive, a threat to the family structure, the Church and the status quo? We can wear our veils. Sometimes we can hide behind them completely, sometimes lift them slightly to reveal only part of what we know. Other times we can joyously wave them around in the air. It's not always easy to know when to do which. It takes practice and instinct and from time to time we're bound to get it wrong. But that's part of learning and becoming comfortable with who we really are.

However, to answer the question How can we embrace Her spirit in a very personal way and use it out in the world? I go back to the source of our wisdom and power—the body, especially "the pelvic mind." When we're dancing, the most important thing to remember is this: All powerful movements come from the center. However we look, and regardless of whether others think our movements are acceptable or not, if we tap the center, we can dance in whatever way we want. But if we fail to connect with the center or respect the messages it sends us, we tumble off-balance and even get hurt. This same principle works in other parts of our lives. When we are confronted, confused, overwhelmed or feel knocked off-balance, we can run decisions through our instincts which go deeper than logic and trust the sensations, positive or negative, that our bodies send as answers. It's that simple. But it's easy to forget.

Awakening carries a responsibility. Becoming a World Dancer lets us use our sacred power and our creative, eccentric senses of humor, rhythm and justice; but it also means we can no longer hide the truth from ourselves. We must tend the magic power inside, use it and believe in it even on days when our power seems to have abandoned us. Once we've let the genie out of the bottle, we can't put her back again. But why would we want to? After we've danced our snaking, curving, spiraling passions across a rounded planet, we can never again see ourselves or the world as flat.

"The center exists everywhere, for in a dance the dancer does not move around an arbitrary point in space, but rather the dance carries its own sense of unity focused around a constantly moving center."

—RACHEL POLLOCK, *Seventy-Eight Degrees of Wisdom, A Book of Tarot*

Our Worlds Collide

I lead a dance class in an aerobics studio above a gym. We always seem to draw crowds of onlookers at the door. Perhaps they are attracted to the music from all over the world or the sight of middle-aged women waving veils in the air. I can't help but notice the different reactions we inspire. Some people walk right through the class, despite the DO NO DISTURB sign on the door, talk in loud voices and treat us as if we don't exist. Some people, mostly women, peek at us from behind the door as if they long to join us but are afraid. Others, usually men, gawk at us as if they've stumbled upon a coven of women engaged in a secret, erotic ritual. They look embarrassed, amused, intimidated. I don't think they understand just *what* they're seeing when they look through that door.

Our reactions are interesting as well. Sometimes we stop dancing, as if we've been "caught in the act," "found out" and might then be hand-tied, shackled and dragged to the pyre. But after many interruptions, we seem to grow a thicker skin over our self-consciousness and keep dancing as if we don't care what anyone thinks. But none of us is immune to distraction.

Dancing in a feminine, spontaneous spirit requires a sense of safety. Before we can let loose enough to dance our full experience, we need to feel that we're in a sanctuary, in a circle of supportive friends and away from critical eyes. But this doesn't always happen either in class or in life. So we have to accept that interruption in various forms: lack of respect, envy, judgment, desire, and others' projections are part of the dance. The hardest part is staying true to the source of the motion and not diluting or exaggerating our movements or emotions once we feel someone watching. Dancing for ourselves and dancing for an audience can be very different experiences. Some dancers come alive in front of a group. Others want to disappear. It is my goal, however unrealistic, to make dancing for ourselves and performing for others very much the same experience, whether we're in class or onstage. When there is an audience, invited or not, our intention is to feel safe enough to dance our passions without seeking approval or being afraid. I would like the audience to feel as if they've happened upon a private, sacred ceremony that they're privileged to watch.

This is easier said than done. I've been dancing for many years alone on beaches and in dance studios and I've always been aware when people walk by, although it gets easier to block them out. I believe that if I choose not to feel awkward when I'm being observed, the observer won't feel as awkward either. I've also performed onstage and have attempted, not always successfully, to imagine that I'm still just dancing for me but am simply revealing my heart in a place where others can read it.

But in the dance studio above the gym, there is still a good deal of awkwardness that results when the world of sacred dance above collides with the world of secular muscle and sweat below. Our confused reactions mirror the very discomfort both sexes feel about openly displayed feminine sacred power. When our observers are men, sometimes our eyes meet and what follows is a long, frozen moment of silence. It's as if we're looking across centuries, across the tundra of a foreign planet, across a battlefield with corpses thousands of years dead. We want to speak but don't know the words. We yearn for a bridge to connect us, a reunion with our lost and wandering other halves just as they crave union with us. But we're all somewhat wary of one another and protected. We want their love and respect but are shy. They want our love, too—so desperately sometimes they can't even admit it to themselves; it's easier for them to laugh and put us down. We don't dare invite them into our circle, not because we don't want to or wouldn't feel safe if they danced with us. It's just that most men wouldn't be caught dead dancing this way. Yet, isn't this what we all so desperately crave—the freedom to dance together—not necessarily in this circle, but in life?

Why Men Need the Goddess

> "It's impossible for the male to see the whole female as holy, he fears all that body stuff, all that blood and emotion in her, dreads facing in himself the things he has learned to demean as female, dreads his vulnerability, his mortality. To be male he thinks he must be fundamentally different from her."
>
> —Elinor Gadon, *The Once and Future Goddess*

The Sacred Feminine is as much a missing piece for men as it is for women. But to men, it's a tough sell—and not one I would push on an average guy. Men usually embrace the power associated with the Divine Feminine only after they've been humbled by life, after failures, loss, illness and/or age have softened their shells (and if they do embrace such a power, they call it another name). They don't die and become reborn every month as we do in our blood cycles, which put us in a constant state of ascension or descent. Consequently, they have to learn such things from scratch.

Men are often both attracted to and repelled by a sacred, sensual, potent femininity. They may admire it in women and yearn to possess a woman who has it but will also ultimately fear and reject her if she has "too much," if she makes their purpose obsolete. It's even harder for them to accept such powers inside themselves. Many men are afraid of intuition, gut knowing and "dying inside to become reborn" because it takes them into unknown territory, into places that can't be charted on spreadsheets or five-year plans. There's no "bottom line" in the Underworld. To admit the mystery and embrace the unknown robs them of their role as warriors, conquering heroes and father-protectors who are supposed to have it all figured out. Wiser men realize, however, that such "feminine" qualities often make them *better* leaders, warriors and protectors because they become more sensitive to the situations around them, less likely to "call in the troops" and charge ahead when it isn't warranted. Such sensitivity adds compassion to reason and intuition to battle, and places more value on humility than victory—all attributes which could, in the long run, bring men more personal and/or worldly power and satisfaction.

Many men are starved of their "female" natures because from an early age they are taught to be tough. They're told that character comes from victory over pain, that being a man comes from doing without. But they're seldom schooled in where to invest their fear, deep feelings, sensibilities for the sacred, for beauty, passion or where to put emotional pain. Thus, when these feelings erupt, few know what to do with them. Such yearnings, especially when they're unmet or unexpressed, often turn first into frustration, then into anger or violence—emotions many men resort to to get things done, fight, score, win, prove their might. To many men, anger is the only acceptable emotion. Going through the world this way often leaves them bruised, dry and hungry for the feminine spirit—which is one reason why they sometimes possessively hang on to women because they don't know how to generate the sweetness in themselves.

I can't help but wonder how the world might be different if more men invoked the power of the Divine Feminine in everyday life:

Would male architects design buildings not only in blueprints but also with a sensitivity to the ground the buildings sit on, the curves in a hillside, the angles of the sun? Would they see that buildings, like women, contain sheltered sacred spaces, even voices that cry out for what details they need for completion?

Might businesses run by men grow not solely on projections and theory but from one day to the next in natural progression, led by people of passion, vision and with experiences that ring down to the bones?

In the gym, would men pass up the urge to lift heavy weights with bad form and instead find wonder in the silent exploration of muscle and sensation, milk wisdom from the lightest weights in the rack? Would they even have the nerve to *dance* with us?

In bed, would men discover how slow, circular gyrations more profoundly arouse the passion of a "sacred prostitute" than simply the old linear, in-and-out thrust?

There *are* men out there who use and appreciate so-called "feminine" attributes like intuition, sensing skills, ethics, balance, regulation of resources, etc. I married one. These men are masculine, successful, intelligent, sexy people who enjoy the company of women. Yet, there seem to be

"In our age of technology, with its emphasis on achievement and control, it is as though the creative phallus has been lost and men have sacrificed their inner daughters to the devil through possessiveness. Frequently they are afraid to acknowledge their wounds and have lost access to their tears."

—LINDA SCHIERSE LEONARD,
The Wounded Woman

many more "bottom-line guys" who don't put much value in such things, who care only about victory, not how the game is played, and are often blind to the beauty, depth and wisdom of the women closest to them. So what can we do about this?

Change *is* under way. The shift toward a humbler, more respectful treatment of the Earth and its resources, our families, our bodies and one another is a mark of the Divine Feminine. Therefore, these "feminine" sacred powers have already begun to affect the lives of those who don't even know that feminine power exists. That, at least, is a start.

In our personal lives, it's perhaps a bit more awkward because many of us don't quite know how to have Her in our lives, be honest about it and also earn the respect of our husbands, fathers, brothers, friends, coworkers. The Goddess, therefore, is still doing some of Her best work in the Underground—in secret, in the shadows. She has come to life again in books, religious gatherings, artwork, public performances and private rituals. She will come out further into the light when it is safe. As for now, I believe that the power of the Divine Feminine will be greater if we don't shout about it or preach but honor it in our own lives and let the magic spread as it may.

The qualities of the feminine are already within men, just as the qualities of the masculine are inside women. These are not new or foreign concepts. The attention has simply shifted back onto the feminine at this time, not because it's better or more important than the masculine but because the patriarchal, militaristic way of doing things has long had its day and its shortcomings are becoming more apparent. The imbalance begs for correction.

It's going to take awhile, perhaps a long time before such sacred power earns a place of importance and respect in business, politics, religion, even at home. But one of the strengths of the receptive, feminine spirit is patience. As we know from history, humans have recognized this power for at least 42,000 years. If *we* hold it sacred and use it at work, at home and at play, we can inspire and inform others without necessarily admitting the source. Eventually, perhaps, others will recognize its radiance and be drawn to it on their own.

Dancing into Cyber Space

As we stand on the threshold of the twenty-first century, it appears that we are ready to leap into an exhaust-free, sweat-free, fiber-optic future where technology is king and hyperfast is the only speed. Some may well ask, Why do we need the soft, round dances of our ancestors? And why the image of the Goddess? Isn't this simply a romantic, reactionary, unrealistic harking back to the Stone Age? What possible use could this be to people in the modern world?

We are awash in a sea of information. We have choices at our fingertips and realities that even a decade ago were beyond comprehension. Everything we want to know seems knowable. Everything we want to possess, we can dial up. We can link up with one another in nanoseconds and through the language of hypertext, find just the right Web site to address our very specific interests and needs (in fact, see Sources!). The cyber future looks safe, clean, cheap and seductive. As we get older, more curious, more crusty and less likely to go out, it will become both our global forum and shopping mall. All we have to do is turn on our "teleputers" and into our personal worlds will fall information, products and services on demand. But the inherent danger is that we could easily live life from the neck up, lose our human *being*ness, favor E-mail over human touch, leave our sacred history in museums and look upon Earth and female-friendly pursuits as quaint or absurdly passé.

Men are more likely to leave the body in favor of the techno-mind (except for sex, of course—cyber or otherwise), since more men are seduced by gadgets, although women are catching up. At least women have vanity and fear of fat to keep bringing us back into our bodies, although not always in a playful manner. But at least we "go there." It is for this reason that we stand a greater chance of sinking down below the cerebral cortex and discovering, even by accident, our gut knowing, even preserving our ancestral wisdom. However, we could easily forget that although our information travels in straight, clear cables faster than our minds can imagine, *our* evolution is still slow and spiraling. Like trees, we, too, earn another ring around our trunks each year and revolve a full cycle around the sun.

Simply embracing "fitness" is no guarantee that we'll preserve the wisdom inherent in our bodies. Fitness now sports its own high-tech jungle. We can find out, via computer, the fitness and diet formula that's "right for us!" We can get printouts of all our bodily functions: blood profiles, optimal body fat content and training heart rates, optimal percentages of calories to consume per day, broken down further into percentages of carbohydrates, proteins and fats. We can get specific computerized instructions on how many workouts to do each week, what type and at what intensity. We can find out how much weight to lift, the number of reps, sets and exercises we need to lose X amount of body fat and gain X amount of strength. To enhance performance, we can have all our movements digitally analyzed: everything from a golf or tennis swing to a swim stroke or running stride. These can be informative tools if we use them to discover more about ourselves, especially if we're training for an athletic event. But we also don't need any of these things if we just want to stay fit. We can use common sense and listen to our bodies. If we grow dependent on our high-tech gadgets to tell us about our bodies, we'll be in danger of traveling further from our feeling centers and, thus, become even more cerebral and less "body-wise." We may think we need sophisticated exercise machines to get a workout, but we forget we are the most sophisticated exercise machines of all.

Dancing in our skin (or any conscious, playful approach to movement) is the simplest, most low-tech, high-spirited way to stay connected with our humanity and our sacred selves, especially as we fly warp speed into the future. Most people I know are already overwhelmed and exhausted. We're worn out from juggling family and work and balancing our materialistic and soul desires. We already make hundreds if not thousands of decisions each day: from the subconscious (such as, "Should I turn this way or that?") to the painstakingly conscious (reading labels, fine print, steering through complex negotiations, trying to follow a computer manual, solve a problem or get a grasp on the course of our lives). By the time we get home and flop in front of the TV, we're in overload—just in time to be bombarded with forty or fifty channels sporting hundreds of commercials with hundreds more choices. Will we feel any *less* overwhelmed with five hundred channels? Will we finally get a handle on life when the information clamoring to get into our heads will multiply by ten, twenty, a hundred times in just the next few years or months? Is there peace to be found despite E-mail, beepers, cell phones, portable faxes and a World Wide Web so densely woven it could possibly take on a conscious mind of its own?

The question I pose is "At what price humanity?" Must we evolve at the expense of the primal, "pelvic mind," the Goddess and the mystery? We need to remember to come back into the body to respect and honor *its* own potent powers, rather than only the power of technology. The information that comes through our computer chips is a stream of 0's and 1's. The information that comes to us through our bodies, is, when broken down to its subatomic essence, a collection of particles and waves with snaking, spiraling, feminine curves! These forms, if we take the time to remember, *are* us.

If we are to embrace this glut of information and stay whole in the process, we need respite in the underground; we need to reexamine the old ways. Only by looking back and reclaiming our "lost" senses can we move forward with greater perspective. We need to know who we were and are in a larger sense and, from time to time, forget who we are in a personal sense, so we can find balance and simplicity in the already-up-and-zooming Information Age. Computers may already be smarter than we are. They may be able to tally up our expenses, draw our pictures, make our movies, compose our songs and perhaps even write our books. But they can't move us with the power of touch; they can't cry and they still can't dance.

9   In Our Power

We don't need the straight line to nowhere. We need the circle to hold us.

We don't need the solitary confinement of modern life; we need the embrace of community.

We can't lose sight, lose faith, courage, forget who we are. We have to remind each other.

We don't need to be warriors. We can be dancers.

The Circle Expands

"Within the eternal circle, the dance of consciousness continues uninterrupted."

—Vicki Noble, *Motherpeace, A Way to the Goddess through Myth, Art and the Tarot*

Most of us travel in parallel lines. We drive in separate lanes mute behind the tempered glass, work at desks lined up in rows, climb up, down, forward and back on our individual stairways to success and map out our one-, five- and ten-year plans for life. We are weak with hunger for the simple power of the circle but don't have time to schedule it in with all our other appointments. Yet this is the very nourishment we need: a gathering of generations, a sense of community where babies are passed from lap to lap so that each child has many mothers and each mother many children, each woman many sisters, mothers, daughters and friends. We need gut laughter, to slip off our girdles and wag our behinds because there's freedom when we're away from men and the guard is down. We need respite from the sun gods, concrete and dependents. We need to nourish ourselves in the wisdom of the circle. We need a place where it's safe to reveal our souls, tell stories, sing and dance for ourselves.

The women's circle used to be a regular part of life. Our grandmothers and mothers had sewing circles, church groups, gardening clubs, where they would turn the chairs to face one another and exchange gossip, recipes, opinions and consolations over coffee and sweets. In the mythology of America, this is still a potent image.

Many women of my generation grew up condemning this tradition. We thought we had more important worlds to conquer outside the circle of women. We wanted to become warriors, hunter-gatherers, heroes, professionals, athletes, intellectuals, artists and, when we could fit it in, daughters, sisters, lovers, mothers, wives. We felt stifled in the quaint, closed-in air of the church basement or the neighbor's kitchen. We needed the whole world—and to have it, sometimes we sacrificed all remnants of femininity, at least those that seemed superficial or weak and would hold us back. We wore low-heeled shoes and tore the lace off our sleeves to adapt and survive. But what have we really won standing alone like soldiers on watch? What have we gained stripping ourselves of softness? What have we proven by lowering ourselves to the bottom line? Have we succeeded in demonstrating the power of *women*? Or have we surrendered our very moisture and become dry as sticks?

Without the circle of one another, we get brittle and break. We have no core, no gut wisdom, no feminine sorcery, no lasting friends. We need to go back to the women's circle and reinvent it to suit today's world. We need to reclaim our magic in the company of one another, so we'll know it's there and we're not crazy. We need to crown ourselves as initiates, "virgins," temple dancers, goddesses, great mothers, wise women, priestesses, shamans or queens so we know where we are in the great cycle of life and thus become more patient and compassionate. Together, we can assist one another to see beyond the details that often drag us down, so we can finally know who we are. There's perhaps no more powerful or delightful group on the planet than a gathering of women who simply tell the truth.

We need to understand down to our bones that we bring a different sort of wisdom to the world: mother love, divine love and the love of the sacred prostitute, everyday energy taken higher with channeled devotion. In the company of one another, we can reclaim our sensuality not as mere set dressing or as a tool, weapon or means of survival but a force that runs through us, the way a river runs through a gorge. This energy determines our perceptions, thoughts, tastes and pleasures and is our magic and our power, which we can use to remake ourselves and the world.

Together, in our kitchens, meeting rooms, church basements and dance studios, we can finally understand down to our fibers that we *are* the missing piece. *We're* what the conquering hordes desired, raped, pillaged and kept trying to squelch when the world switched from matriarchy to patriarchy. But we're no longer the victims; we're the cure. We are, as Joseph Campbell said, already *there*; we *are* the place people are trying to get to. And what is that place? It is an intelligent, sexual, expressive, creative, funny, sensitive, divine, fully alive balance of forces.

Inside the circle, we can dress up for one another, notice the details, finery and effort that men often miss; or we can come into it with a naked face and all our weariness. Either way, we can be seen for who we are; we can be sensed, heard, felt, respected. We speak not only in words but also in tones of voice, colors, the placement of food on a plate, aromas, textures, touch, rhythms and motions. Each one of us possesses at least one divinely feminine instinct to such a great capacity, we could turn it into not only a fulfilling passion but also a thriving *business*. Should we discover that we can no longer tolerate old structures and have to pull the rip cord on stifling jobs or marriages in order to fully blossom, these skills can both save and redefine our lives. In the circle of friends, we find our first and most loyal customers and each of them has another circle of friends.

The circle is expanding because more of us need its healing medicine. We've come home from the front banged up, broken, tired and sick. Knowing how to fight and be tough are useful skills during floods, famines, war and personal crises. But we don't have to fight all the time. Our souls don't find nourishment in lines of militaristic precision; they find it in the circle.

People will ask, "What's with this Goddess thing? It sounds so trendy." The answer is simple. No one ever asks if God is a trend. We seek guidance from One with a face, body and emotions we can relate to and we want to embody Her spirit. People have done this throughout history. Embracing the Goddess doesn't mean we then must reject God or traditional religion. On the contrary: some of us have found that the Goddess opens a *new* door, leading us back to our original religious upbringings, but with an entirely different, expanded spirit. The Divine Feminine is a personal thing—different, no doubt, for each of us. She is a voice inside, a state of being to strive for, an energy so overwhelming we can't comprehend it and

"In the whole mythological tradition, the woman is *there*. All she has to do is to realize that she's the place that people are trying to get to. When a woman realizes what her wonderful character is, she's not going to get messed up with the notion of being pseudo-male."

—MAUREEN MURDOCK, *The Heroine's Journey* (interview with Joseph Campbell)

"A true transformation of our culture would require reclaiming the erotic as power-from-within, as empowerment. The erotic can become the bridge that connects feeling with doing."

—STARHAWK, *Dreaming the Dark, Magic, Sex and Politics*

a soft place of retreat in a world that's hard. She has many faces, is all ages and does many different jobs. She is as much at home in overalls digging in the mud as she is dancing with veils.

People will also ask, "Why do you dance around in circles? Is this some weird kind of ritual? If you want to exercise, why not just get on the stair climber?" The answer is simple here, too. The circle satisfies both a body yearning and a soul desire at the same time. In the soft dances, the body itself seems to become more sacred; potent energies are released. Through the vehicle of soft motions, we are not trying to tame, burn or shrink ourselves. We're trying to feel our essence and the power that dwells within. The circle not only gives a shape to our movements; it is *our* shape, whether it folds back on itself or curves off in a spiral or snake. It pays homage to the bulbous curve of our breasts, the round softness of our bellies, buttocks and thighs and to the snaking, spiraling, meandering movements of organic life on Mother Earth. We *are* the circle and all it contains—and the circle contains all shapes equally within its perimeter.

Reembracing the circle is part of our awakening. If enough of us recognize the power of the circle, it will rise out of the ancient ashes and work its way into our modern mythology. It is the shape of all things being equal. Inside it, no one is ahead of or behind another. Inside the circle, we are all parts of the whole.

A Legacy for Lost Daughters

There is a whole new generation of little girls (and boys) growing up lost in America. Drug use among teens has recently doubled. Teenage smoking is cool again and at an all-time high, while regular participation in exercise is at an all-time low. Eating disorders have become rampant even among girls in elementary school. There's more pressure on teens than ever to match the current ideals, which have become even more impossible and extreme: from the starving-waif supermodel who looks as though she just snorted a line of coke, to the Ms. Fitness supervixen without an ounce of fat on her body. It's very hard to be normal and acknowledge all the forms that "normal" can take. Many teenage girls no longer want only clear skin and fashionable clothes. They want plastic surgery, breast implants and big hair—or in my neighborhood, pierced navels, blue hair and bell bottoms that drift off their hips. They're not only falling into the same traps many of us fell into: losing their nerve at puberty, courting unconsciousness in food binges, drugs and alcohol, having unsafe sex with people who don't appreciate them and scorning their reflections for the worst of all possible fates—fat! They're falling into *deeper* traps: the drugs are more dangerous, the predators are more frightening, the diseases more deadly, even the remedies for body loathing are more destructive. Those who tumble into the Underworld, stripped of their first layer of sacred power, are at even greater risk of not making it out.

Those of us who grew up in the sixties and seventies can't help but see ourselves reflected in them. They've even adopted our tie-dyed hippie look, our disco platform shoes and our old devils, too: marijuana, alcohol, heroin, cocaine, LSD. How many of *us* have since found our way back home? How many of us have since recovered, found our voices, our own dances, two legs to stand on and a femininity that feels true? If we haven't at our age, what are the chances they will? Yes, they find us lacking in many ways, even boring in our conversions to exercise and low-fat living. But we're what they've got for mothers, aunts, fairy godmothers and big sisters. To them, we represent the road ahead, whether they imitate us, rebel against us or both.

I once gave a talk on women's muscle and strength to a group of high school girls and practically got booed off the stage. I was asked to speak because the vice principal told me that roughly *75 percent* of them had some degree of eating disorder! She told me that what they needed was simple truth about bodies, exercise, food and self-esteem. I showed them slides of beautiful women throughout the ages with all different body types. I gave them statistics about how exercise in general could help give them a sense of balance with food, more of a natural respect and greater awareness of their bodies (as opposed to rigid control), give them energy (many complained of extreme lethargy), burn fat and conquer mental demons as well. I told them how exercise can help lessen the odds of succumbing to the lures of drug use and teenage pregnancy; and I mentioned the boring benefits (at least to them) of bone strength and discipline. One of the girls raised her hand and said, "We already have enough pressures on us to look a certain way. Now we're supposed to be buffed, too?" "No," I said, "just *active*." I wanted them to respect their bodies, find movement they loved, not feel they *should* do, but *want* to do so they could achieve long-term health. But they heard the word *muscle* and got stuck there, as many people do. What I had to say sounded too much like a sermon. Only a few of the already converted—the soccer players, rowers, basketball players and swimmers—agreed that there are many gifts that grow when feminine muscle meets movement.

"For many women, the root of their injury stems from a damaged relationship with the father. They may have been wounded by a bad relation to their personal father, or wounded by the patriarchal society which itself functions like a poor father, culturally devaluing the worth of women."

—LINDA SCHIERSE LEONARD,
The Wounded Woman

I believe the Goddess is an easier sell. Myths and stories about goddesses do not preach formulas for health and happiness, mention optimal daily intake of calories and fat, numbers of reps or workouts to do each week or revere one body type above all others and therefore feed a sense of hopelessness and inadequacy. Goddess myths instead focus on courage, the search for knowledge, individuality and self-expression. They teach us that there are other forms of salvation besides being born rich, genetically blessed or rescued by princes. Goddesses are shown as independent but seeking intimate love, compassionate and vulnerable but also fierce and strong. They may have difficult histories with their mothers and fathers but they're able to overcome, forgive, become their own women and form loving relationships with them in the end. They seldom need men to feel complete, loved, worthy. Yet they'll go literally to the ends of the Earth, into the Underworld to bring life back to one they love. When they need to survive, they can sustain themselves on almost nothing. But to thrive over the long term, they need food, love, a place to channel their creative energies, encouragement and support.

We need to tell young women the myths of the Goddess so they, too, can understand and honor who they are in a larger context beyond friends, school and parents. They need to see themselves, just as we do, reflected in a glass that goes back further than their birth time so they can embrace the gift of being born in a woman's body, in a world that desperately needs a wise woman's ways. These myths also offer guidance in a time that is barren of instructive storytelling, particularly for young people.

We need to invite our daughters into our circles, so they can seek wisdom from women *besides* their mothers, whom they don't listen to much of the time anyway. This way, when they rebel against the mother, they don't hold all women in contempt and therefore reject their own inherent feminine power. The best thing we can do is just show them a group of women of all ages, celebrating ourselves as we are. We can teach them, by example, that self-acceptance doesn't mean that once we realize we can't change certain things, we roll over and play dead. On the contrary, it makes us more excited about living, more motivated to look within for greater self-understanding, more intent on preserving our vitality through regular, joyful, physical activity.

Young women seem instinctively drawn to a tribal way of life. They dress alike, travel in packs, love adornment and ceremony. They are naturals for the women's circle. In a women's circle—and not just a circle of their peers—they are more likely to see the value of cultivating their individual perspectives and style even during an age when the pull is toward conformity and fitting in.

Young women are also naturals for a *dance* circle. But the type of dance we leave them need not be full of rigid dress codes, body-type requirements or moves that separate the "hopefuls" from the "hopeless." We can offer a looser structure, a formula rather than a strict form—one that offers both discipline and spontaneity, strength and grace, exercise and fun *and* provides a balance of both individual expression and respect for the group. I cannot help but wonder how many more young women might be seduced into healthy habits if they could dance in a way that feels right for *their* bodies, rather than feeling hopelessly uncoordinated if they can't master a particular dance style or sport. I wonder how many more would come to dance in colorful, feminine clothing rather than run around in ugly gym uniforms. I wonder, too, how many would sign up if such dancing also provided a safe expression of their budding sexuality and darker emotions as well: rage, jealousy, laziness, fear, obsessive desires, grief and the cool blue swells of depression—emotions that many grown women don't know what to do with.

Do we want to leave a legacy of shame about our bodies or exercise as penance for overindulgence? Do we want young women to associate exercise with torture and believe we should hide our fat under oversized T-shirts? On the other hand, do we want them to think that being fit lets us parade around in little thongs and midriffs, grab attention and show off our goods? Or do we want to show them that movement is a pleasure, a natural, primal desire within each of us—and that we can all find something we enjoy? Wouldn't we rather teach them that being healthy helps us connect to the body's wisdom and that dancing can teach us respect for our rich, deep, sacred femininity?

Perhaps it will be our daughters and their daughters who will bring the fully realized power of the Sacred Feminine out of the dark and into the light of day. Perhaps they will be the ones to restore soft, feminine motions to a place of prayer. Perhaps they will lead the world to honor feminine sexuality and its divine heritage. But it is our job as elders to set the stage and carry the evolution forward as far as we can, so they can see over our shoulders. It's our job as mothers, seers and triple goddesses to make them aware of *their* powers, the powers born of women who need care and watering or they might never bloom.

Inching Toward Our (R)Evolution

"Myths may lie dormant and inert for millennia, like the virus, until the "chemical" time is right for them to exteriorise into rational fact."

—Lawrence Blair,
Rhythms of Vision

Interest in the wisdom of the Divine Feminine is appearing at the end of the twentieth century as if to guide us back to a part of ourselves that we once naturally possessed but had lost and forgotten. In order to move forward as whole beings into the third millennium and preserve our sanity, the status of women and the planet, we must once again cultivate this wisdom. We all possess and need both the female and male principles, just as much as we need the moon and the sun. This book, for instance, was written as much in darkness and dreams as it was in the light of day. The chaotic, illogical, predawn muses were just as important as the noonday, level-headed critic with outlines and red pen. Without the dark, there would have been no juice. Without the clear light of day, there would have been no order. But we can't achieve such a balance of forces on a large scale until we first restore the power of the Divine Feminine to Her former place of honor—first in our private lives and then in public.

These terms *feminine* and *masculine*, also *sacred* and *secular*, *logic* and *intuition*, *right brain* and *left*, even *the Goddess* and *God* all seem to be opposites. However, there's but the thinnest of membranes between them—and a large gray area where they seem to be the same. Yet throughout history we've polarized these forces and fought to the death over which is better or right, just as we have fought over which culture or religion is superior—a no-win war. Neither side is better. But our modern world still places greater value on the secular, the left brain, logic and Father God. Until more people honor the sacred, the right brain, intuition and a Mother God, we won't be in balance. The shift *is* happening, but it's slow.

Many of us have begun to realize that when we try to impose too much rigid order on our bodies, children, other people, on the land, even on our schedules, we fail. We fail because we don't factor in the unpredictable and unknown, the X factor, the magic, another powerful hand at work. We don't sway with the forces. We hold ourselves as a supreme authority and are surprised when what we're trying to control rebels. Then we end up disappointed, frustrated or perhaps more determined than ever to exert *ultimate* control. After all, we have to maintain order, don't we? We can't just swirl around in chaos, always living, moment to moment, according to how we feel. We've got schedules to maintain, bills to pay, structures to build. But we *can* create order without stifling the living exuberant spirit within. Finding such a balance between these two approaches, between control and surrender, is an ongoing dance.

As we age and get pulled closer to death, we confront the huge, gaping Wonderland of our soul's passage. This is the territory of the Divine Feminine, and we are all eventually pulled here in one way or another. So the question is, How do we want to confront this—in curiosity or fear? If we learn not to fear our own illogical, dark places, we can find treasure in our own unfolding. As many of us have discovered, some of our greatest insights come in dreams or in the emptiness that follows hard work. Feminine sacred power comes from that place just beyond reason, in that gap between wakefulness and sleep, in that moment when we turn away from the mirror, stop watching the clock, put the technique aside and let the dances come.

Women are carriers of this shift in consciousness because it's natural for us to process emotions and decisions through our intuitive bodies. Men have been more intensely schooled in the superiority of deductive reasoning and therefore haven't been told to trust "gut feelings" as often as women have. If we hold such "knowing" in a place of honor and blend this

"I believe that ideas in human society spread the same kind of way and that when enough of us hold something to be true, then it becomes true for everyone."

—LYALL WATSON, Foreword to *Rhythms of Vision*

"Women need to breathe more knowledge, more prana into the world to restore the imbalance. We *are* a pilgrim people, we are on a journey *together* to learn how to honor and preserve the dignity of all life forms seen and unseen; therein lies our heroic power."

—Maureen Murdock, *The Heroine's Journey*

ability with logic and the bottom line, it will gain even more respect. We'll speak in a language more will understand. What keeps us polarized and warring over the superiority of "opposite" forces is when we hold only one half of the equation as *the* entire answer. Our (r)evolution will no doubt include integrating these two seemingly distinct states of learning and knowing into a unified whole, a blend of spirit and science.

Tapping the power of the Sacred Feminine can be very confusing sometimes. Once we've expanded into a greater sense of ourselves, it's hard to shrink back to a size others find more acceptable. After we've experienced a sense of timelessness, it's hard to schedule back-to-back appointments. After we've swished our hips in jangling scarves, it feels absurd to throw jabs and punches. Yet our power will have greater influence if we keep a foot in both worlds. We need to stay flexible so, like the World Dancer, we are comfortable dancing in all realms.

Global acceptance of the Sacred Feminine, especially when it is embodied by mere mortal women like us, won't be linear and direct. It will come in waves, die down (be shot down) and come again, in a spiral pattern. Just when we think that our (r)evolution is well under way, the ax of the patriarchy may aim to chop off our dancing feet. We may be fueled by enthusiasm, unity and a sense of being "in our power" and suddenly find ourselves snared in a trap, out of a job or growing out of a stifling situation. It can still be very discouraging out there, if not dangerous. But if we cultivate our sacred power, we'll always hold on to a part of ourselves that is beyond the reach of criticism. If we remember that our own evolutions are spiraling, full of returnings, rememberings, losses, unexpected pleasures and lessons learned many times, we can ride through rough phases with greater compassion for ourselves and others. With each ring of the spiral we acquire more knowledge—and with more of us moving in this direction, perhaps evolution itself will speed up.

As more women move into both sacred and secular power, we must remember that although we're all trying to survive, do our work and also perhaps achieve recognition and the money we deserve, we don't need to conquer *one another* in the process. This is not our style. Our competition can be healthy and friendly. Our method is tribal. Our geometry is the circle. Our power increases when we support one another.

As the myths of the Goddess inform us, the stories of our lives have not changed all *that* much throughout the centuries, only the details. The dance of the ancient dancer on a Mesopotamian hilltop is not much different from that of a modern-day goddess in a studio on Main Street. We're dancing the same stories over and over, whether we realize it or not. But whether we dance alone or in the circle, to modern songs or ancient rhythms, to capture the spirit of our own times, touch the past or shape the future, we are weaving our bodies, hearts and spirits into one. The wholeness we create completes not only our own lives but also the lives of all women who have ever longed to enter that "place of the dance."

Here we aren't held back by age or ability. There is no effort to expend, no planning or worry. In one moment, we leave ourselves and become ourselves more completely than ever before. Like the sacred dancer throughout time, we focus not on how we look but on the power of the dance. Every footfall lands just as we want it to. Every gesture trembles with meaning. When others watch us, they see that we are dancing their feelings and their stories, too, and they weep and howl yet often don't know why. We are *driven* to paint our history on the air. This doesn't feel like a choice. We are being guided, all moving in the same direction. We are dancing the Divine Feminine back into the world.

Addendum—Sources

Carolena Nericcio,
Director,
FatChanceBellyDance

Many of us are doing work inspired or informed by the Sacred Feminine: in the arts, in business, in groups, in our personal lives, out in the open and partially or fully veiled. Here is a small but by no means complete list of sources for soul-inspired *movement*. Some are ethnically precise. Some, like my own, are a blend of influences: different dance styles, fitness, martial arts, yoga, ritual and/or theater. Others have no distinct origin at all. The beauty is there's room for every style, method, individual voice and vision.

FatChanceBellyDance
Carolena Nericcio

When I first saw the troupe FatChanceBellyDance perform at a belly dance festival, I felt that I was finally seeing, in person, the spirit of dance I'd been searching for. The dancers seemed to embody our womanly magnificence as it used to be, before we worried about scaring others with our stature, editing our power, copying the current idols of beauty—or before worry itself stripped away our elegance. In their gorgeous gypsy costumes with bright satin pantaloons peeking out from under rustling skirts, their queenly turbans crowned with flowers and beads, their jangling coin bras, jewels, fringe and veils hanging from every imaginable place, they represented a primal beauty that doesn't wash off, diminish with age or fade as fashions change. In them, I saw the reflection of all of *us*: all races, ages and body types—each one radiant in her own right. As they danced and celebrated themselves, they celebrated all of us. Their dances seemed to say "You, too, can have this. In fact, you already have it." After the festival, I immediately signed up for class.

Carolena Nericcio is the founder, essence and force behind the San Francisco–based FCBD. One of the things I have found most remarkable about studying with Carolena is that her embodiment of the Goddess is mostly unconscious. She didn't set out to represent the Divine Feminine. She simply does—and does it with such natural grace, it's as if she had been born directly into her Queendom and, along the way, never forgot who she was.

FCBD performs "American tribal-style belly dance." They didn't create this phrase; it was created for them, to distinguish their style from a specific tribe and because no one knew what else to call it. Nonetheless, it seems appropriate because it describes a combination of influences. Their movements have the entertaining quality of cabaret-style belly dance and the simple earthiness of folkloric. Cabaret or "nightclub style" is glittery, full of intricate, quick changes, has a lighter feel to it and is especially well suited for solo work. Folkloric draws its roots more from communal folk dance and has a heavier feel to it, with more weight in the legs. Its movements are "painted" with simpler, broader strokes so that everyone can do them. FatChanceBellyDance has an American *athletic* quality as well, a strong physical dimension, due in part to the fact that Carolena herself lifts weights and is all-over fit and, therefore, aware not simply of the *show* side of dance but also the kinesiology, the function beneath the form. Dancing this style is a subtle but richly rewarding athletic experience which, like Tai Chi, can become a pleasurable lifelong practice—and one that lubricates the spirit as much as it does the joints.

Dancing tribal style involves learning movement patterns and rules so that everyone can actually improvise together. The result is not only a uniformity in movement but also group communication. All chest circles move counter-clockwise, all Egyptian walks begin with the right hip and all major changes of direction are preceded by a signal. Thus, it's possible to move together spontaneously without words and change directions without telegraphing it in advance. Some dancers find such "rules" limiting to free expression (they might find more individual happiness in cabaret style). But in fact, the tribal-style movement vocabulary forms the core of group dynamics—and thus serves as a metaphor for working in a community. Since ours is more of an individual culture, we don't necessarily know *how* to work together as a tribe. Here, we learn this lesson with our *bodies*. Many of us find it comforting and liberating rather than confining. It's like belonging to an extended family. Even the soloists are backed by a supportive half circle of dancers.

Each class is broken down to two simple moves: one slow, one fast. After about eight weeks of even just one class a week, Carolena has covered almost every basic move, although there's always more to learn. This simplicity is powerful and gives FatChanceBellyDance its resonant, individual style which creates an almost hypnotic effect on the audience.

Carolena has turned FCBD into a successful business. The catalogue features several videos: from "Tribal Basics 1 & 2" to more advanced workshops, there are also videos on costuming and performances. There is an extensive collection of music, books, jewelry, cosmetics, accessories and exquisitely gorgeous clothing—everything the beginning tribal-style belly dancer would want all in one place.

The clothing is lovingly handmade by Gwen Heckeroth of Flying Skirts,

San Francisco. The full balloon pants, three-tiered skirts, short tops (called cholis) and fringed and tasseled hip scarves come in a variety of fabrics and colors. (Carolena's costume on page 175 and my fringed hip scarf, featured in the exercise photos, are all Gwen's "children.") All fabrics are "movable" soft silks, cottons, satins, rayons or velvets, dyed the color of gemstones and all are reasonably priced. Cosmetics featured in the catalog are by FCBD troupe member Suzanne Elliot. Her "Gypsy Queen Anointing Oil" is a spicy, intoxicating scent I wear to remember the magic.

For more information on the catalogue, classes, workshops, performances and a newsletter called "Tribal Talk,"

call: (415) 647-6035
write: FatChanceBellyDance, P.O. Box 460594, San Francisco, CA 94146
visit the Web site: http://www.dnai.com/~ash/FCBD/
or send e-mail to: fcbd@sirius.com

Middle Eastern Dance Video Sourcebook
Donna Carlton

This is a wonderful resource with all sorts of information on dance with a sacred bent. There are videos on all styles of belly dance—cabaret, folkloric and everything in between, featuring well-known teachers and performers. There are also videos on flamenco, hula and Polynesian, plus extensive sources for costumes for all these dance styles. Donna Carlton is the editor of the *Sourcebook*, as well as the author of *Looking for Little Egypt* (IDD Books—see Bibliography and below), a detailed look at "the not-so-innocent era of ballyhoo, sideshows and hootchie-kootchie entertainers who fascinated and scandalized audiences of the day." Donna also has a Web site and e-mail address devoted to dance as "a transformative experience, a spiritual healing and/or karmic journey." Add your voice to the mix.

To order the catalog, book or add your comments, contact:

Middle Eastern Dance Video Sourcebook
International Dance Discovery
Donna Carlton, Editor/Publisher
108 1/2 East Kirkwood Ave. #5

Bloomington, IN 47401
Tel. (812) 336-3632
E-mail: 73261.1065@compuserve.com
Web site: http://ourworld.compuserve.com/homepages/IDD

NIA
Debbie and Carlos Rosas

Debbie and Carlos Rosas are the creators of NIA (Neuromuscular Integrative Action—see page 72). This barefoot, low-impact blend of dance styles and martial arts (with touches of Feldenkrais and Alexander work) was created, as Debbie says, "to dissolve the boundary between the masculine and the feminine. But it grew from planting the seeds of the feminine." It blends soft, circular motions with harder, more linear warrior moves from martial arts—to enhance, as they say, both "guts and grace." This helps bring both the logical and intuitive sides of our bodies and brains into balance. NIA movements all feel gentle on the body and can be adapted to suit each person's level of fitness and movement skill. It's a dance class that satisfies both the sensibilities of dancers and the movement fantasies of "secret dancers," since the moves are all clean, clear and within almost everyone's grasp.

Years ago, when fast tempos, high-impact aerobics, calorie expenditure and hard buns were king, Debbie and Carlos bravely presented their work at fitness conventions and spoke about the body, spirit and mind long before such things were fashionable. They used music with a human touch when everyone else was using computer-generated disco. The fact that their approach to movement still looks and feels current long after other fitness modes have faded out of fashion, shows that Debbie and Carlos have touched upon something timeless and universal. NIA now has over three hundred and fifty trained instructors teaching in at least thirty states in about two hundred facilities—and the numbers are growing. To find out about an NIA class in your area call:

(800) 762-5762.

Sweat Your Prayers, the Five Rhythms
Gabrielle Roth

Gabrielle Roth was one of the first to dream primal dance-as-prayer back into being and introduce it to "nondancers" and Western minds. She began over thirty-five years ago and has since "taken thousands of people on a journey from physical and emotional inertia to the freedom of ecstasy," a journey that she herself has taken and to which she has committed her life.

Gabrielle has an impressive body of work: Her movement practice, the Five Rhythms™, is a "pilgrimage of self-revelation," a combination of tribal rhythms, trance dancing and ritual theater, which, as Gabrielle says, "seduces the soul back into the body." These Five Rhythms are what she calls "universal energies": Flow, Staccato, Chaos, Lyrical and Stillness are the emotional energies, she believes, that we each possess to a certain degree. The ones that feel most difficult to do may in fact have the most to teach us. The idea is that if we dance our emotions, they change; they can even take us into a state of ecstasy.

Gabrielle Roth is also an accomplished musician. Along with her dance/theater/music company, The Mirrors, she has recorded several CDs of primal rhythms and relaxing "songs of stillness," conducive to guiding dancers on inner journeys (see "Dance Music" at the end of this chapter).

She is the author of *MAPS TO ECSTASY: Teachings of an Urban Shaman* (Nataraj Publishing, Mill Valley, Calif., 1989). Her new book, *Sweat Your Prayers: Unveiling the Mysteries of the Soul*, is due in 1998 (Tarcher/Putnam, New York; 1998).

Regular "Sweat Your Prayers" gatherings are held in various parts of the country and led by trained instructors. For more information about workshops or any of the work listed above, contact:

The Moving Center
P.O. Box 2885
Petaluma, CA 94953
Phone: (415) 388-5533
Fax: (707) 773-1263
Web site: http://ravenrecording.com

Continuum
Emilie Conrad D'Oud

Emilie Conrad D'Oud's brainchild, Continuum, drew its inspiration from the amniotic original pool of life—water. In her brochure she states that "our fluid ancestry informs us with movements that curve, arc and spiral . . . Organismic movements integrate and inform in ways that linear, mechanical movements rarely do."

Emilie's work is based on the belief that such movements, along with breath and sound, "awaken creativity, mediate disease processes . . . and revitalize static states" by encouraging "a rapport with that wisdom that swims in our cells." The physical impact of this approach to movement helps combat disease, the emotional impact helps "melt defensiveness" and the spiritual impact tunes us in to the great "matrix of fundamental movement" that "spawns protoplasm, humans and galaxies."

One of her most recent additions to the Continuum curriculum is "Jungle Gym—Frontiers of Movement," a workout that "creates muscular strength through changing relationships with gravity." The strengthening moves not only are linear, as in traditional strength training, but also involve twisting and turning while moving one's own body weight. The *body* becomes the weight machine and the movements not only promote muscular strength but also stimulate connective tissue and "electric conductivity."

With her partner, Susan Harper, and other trained Continuum teachers, Emilie Conrad D'Oud teaches workshops all over the world as well as in her studio in Santa Monica, California. Workshops cover a broad range of topics and include (but aren't limited to) teacher training. There is also a nationwide network of Continuum instructors.

To find out about workshops and classes, contact:

Continuum
1629 18th St., #7
Santa Monica, CA 90404
Office: (310) 453-4402
Fax: (310) 453-8775
E-mail address: continuummove@earthlink.net
Web site: http://www.earthlink.net/ ~ continuummove

Motivity
Terry Sendgraff

Terry Sendgraff is a pioneer of aerial dance—and some of her quirky and inspired aerial creations include trapeze dancing, bungee *dancing* (not jumping off a bridge!) and walking on stilts. Terry seems most at home in the ethers, playfully defying the pull of gravity by achieving every dancer's dream—leaping into the air and staying there! Terry is a performing artist and teacher with a huge heart—one of the most delightful, compassionate, loving teachers around.

Terry's low-flying trapeze hangs just within reach of the floor, so there is no major fear of heights to conquer here. The ropes also come together in a point, so that you don't just swing back and forth like in the circus, you can *spin, spin and spin* for as long as your stomach will allow. But it's not all spinning and swinging. There are countless ways to hang—from ankles, knees, elbows, fingers, one limb and two, also climbing and using two, three or more trapezes at once. Dancing in the air is bliss in motion. The body also looks incredibly graceful and swanlike off the floor. Working on the trapeze doesn't require much upper-body strength or bravery. What it takes is a curiosity to explore momentum. You discover right away that you have to go *with* the momentum, even when you're trying to influence it—otherwise you hit its wall of resistant force. The trapeze responds best to subtle changes of weight—not big, swooping pushes and pulls. The emotional transformation that occurs when people go airborne is immediate. It's like being a bird and leaving the world of crawling beasts behind.

Bungee dancing is also delicious (although these days Terry teaches this on a private and limited basis). Bungee cords hang suspended from the ceiling, and you hook them with carabiners onto a climbing belt (which you wear on the hips). The bungees let you jump five to ten feet off the ground or simply hover, like Peter Pan, in a horizontal position a few feet off the floor (depending on your weight). As with the trapeze, bungee dancing lets you discover momentum from a new perspective. Every action causes a definite and sometimes exaggerated reaction. The ultimate teacher is physics.

Terry's stilt-walking performance, "Women Walking Tall," featured over seventy-five tribal-painted, fringe-legged, drum-banging, chanting, ten-foot-tall women, some bare-breasted, some not—definitely women who embodied sacred power! Terry often teaches workshops in stilt walking in conjunction with trapeze. As you can see, the theme that runs through all of Terry's work encourages women to stand tall, fly high and launch our lives into new dimensions.

Terry is over sixty years old and still dancing (more slowly, but with all her grace intact). She is a survivor of two bouts with breast cancer. After the second bout, she created a trapeze performance piece called "Hovering," in which she celebrated both her life and the wisdom she gained from looking into the eyes of death. She performed the piece nearly naked, dressed only in a G-string, with flames of fire painted where one breast used to be. The work celebrated her survival and also revealed the peace she felt about her body after the surgery. This was, as you can imagine, a ritual healing for Terry and for the audience as well.

Terry's classes and workshops are held in Oakland, Calif., at 530 E. 8th Street. Phone interviews are necessary for enrollment in all her workshops. For information about Terry Sendgraff and Motivity, call:

(510) 482-4729.

Life in Motion
Bruce and Elizabeth Andes Bell

Life in Motion is not so much a dance or movement form but a guided movement *experience*. There is no technique. Therefore, this is a perfect venue for people who long to do body-based "soul work" but are turned off by dance.

Bruce and Elizabeth Andes Bell head the Creative Arts Department of the Barbara Brennan School of Healing, where this work was first introduced to large groups of people in the form of "ecumenical healing ceremonies with shamans of many cultures." But both also have extensive backgrounds in dance and fitness (they own Life in Motion Fitness Club in New York City), teach theatrical movement at the State University of New York Purchase, have healing practices in New York City and Nyack, New York (and are the parents of two children).

These one-and-one-half-hour workshops draw not from a specific school of movement but from "deep contact with the self," the result of focusing on the "pulse of breath and evoking a trance state through music and voice." Every class is different, depending on the group, although there are many recurring themes, such as: uniting male and female energies, exploring the primal self, accessing the core of one's essence. One "goal," if you could call it that, is to allow people to be seen as they are, to be themselves and be witnessed by the group, without judgment.

Bruce and Elizabeth Andes Bell believe that by accessing the "creative wave moving through us at all times," life problems shrink in significance and "one experiences standing in the presence of grace."

To find out about workshops, contact:

Life in Motion, Inc.
P.O. Box 249
New York, NY 10028
(914) 365-4012
E-mail: A&B Bell @ MSN.com

Dance Music

Here are a few sources of dance music that fuse cultures, centuries, melodic harmonies and changeable rhythms. Not all are easily available at your local music store, so you may need to special-order or go to alternative or New Age stores.

Ashik, *Dancing Lightly,* Dancing Leaf Music, 1705 14th St., #224, Boulder, CO 80502, phone and fax (505) 546-6005.
Ashik plays fiddle music with a distinct gypsy feel, capturing the soulful, rich, lusty sounds of Ireland, Hungary, Russia and the rural U.S. Each song has a multirhythmic, textured feel, good for full-range expression.

Baka Beyond, *The Melting Pool,* Rykodisc, Shetland Park, 27 Congress Street, Salem, MA 01970.
This is a playful blend of African melodies meeting Celtic and Cajun, gypsy, Arabic and jazz. Some highly danceable cuts, both rhythmic and serene. Their first release, *Spirit of the Forest*, is another joyful blend of cultures.

Joe Craven, *Camptown.* Acorn Music. Berkeley, CA. 1-800-74-ACORN (742-2676). Web site: http://www.sirius.com/~acorn. E-mail:acorn@ sirius.com.

This is a highly playful, exceedingly danceable combination of nearly every major World beat imaginable. Joe combines African, Celtic, Aboriginal, Middle Eastern, Indian, Cuban, Brazilian, Reggae and old familiar tunes (like "Camptown Races") in very creative ways. He primarily plays fiddle and mandolin but also does a wild turn on a mayonnaise jar and cheese grater! The music on this first solo release not only makes you move, it makes you laugh.

FatChanceBellyDance, *Music for Tribal Basics,* composed for FCBD by Nancy Hall. Contact FCBD at P.O. Box 460594, San Francisco, CA 94146, (415) 647-6035. Web site: http://www.dnai.com/~ash/FCBD/

This is a sampling of different Middle Eastern rhythms with drums, other percussive instruments and finger cymbals. No vocals or melodies. Excellent for teaching, learning and performing.

Gabrielle Roth and the Mirrors, *Initiation,* Raven Recording, P.O. Box 2034, Red Bank, NJ 07701.

This is one of Gabrielle's earliest CDs and a classic. In this recording, she explores the *sounds* of the Five Rhythms. Side B features another piece called "Body Jazz," which is *the* perfect warm-up song. Its seven sections move from "Head" to "Feet" with everything in between. Good, steady tempo for exercise and playful, meandering melodies.

Steven Halpern and Suru, *Afro-Desia,* Open Channel Sound Co. (BMI), Steven Halpern's Inner Peace Music, P.O. Box 2644, San Anselmo, CA 94979-2644, 1-800-909-0707. Web site: http://innerpeacemusic.com.

Steven Halpern fans, more familiar with his gentle, less rhythmic music might be surprised to hear this primal rhythmic work. It's a blend of West African rhythms, with jazz and New Age. Many of the cuts maintain a steady rhythm (but a wandering playful melody), which is very useful for teaching.

Brent Lewis, *Rhythm Hunter,* Ikauma Records, Brent Lewis Productions, P.O. Box 428, Joshua Tree, CA 92252, (619) 366-9540.

Brent Lewis plays Ikauma drums, his own creation of twenty-two "chromatically tuned drums." The sound is tonal, liquid and rich. On this and other various recordings, like *Earth Tribe Rhythms*, he combines African, Aboriginal, Cuban and Middle Eastern rhythms. Brent Lewis is pure percussion—no vocals involved.

Light Rain, *Dark Fire,* Magi Productions, P.O. Box 356, Larkspur, CA 94977, (415) 892-0181.
Light Rain's music blends the sultry, dreamy quality of "Arabian Nights" with quick, fiery, gypsy tempos. Their other releases, *Dream Dancer, Dream Suite* and *Valentine to Eden* contain music that has been used by the Joffrey and Oakland ballets.

Lorenna McKennitt, *The Mask and the Mirror,* Warner Brothers, 1994, 3300 Warner Blvd., Burbank, CA 91505-4694 and 75 Rockefeller Plaza, New York, NY 10019-6908.
This is the ultimate blend of Celtic and Middle Eastern. The first time I heard this, I broke into tears. Lorenna McKennitt's harp and voice seem to sing through all time. She is not just a musician but a visionary. Buy this. Every song is magnificent. Her other best-selling CD, *The Visit*, features "Tango to Evora," which was the soundtrack for *The Burning Times*, a documentary by Canadian filmmaker Donna Read about the blackest time in women's history. (Donna Read's three documentaries are must-see films for anyone interested in the Goddess and women's spiritual history. This trilogy includes: *The Goddess Remembered, The Burning Times* and *Full Circle.* All were sponsored by the National Film Board of Canada. Many are also for sale or rent via "alternative bookstores" and also play on PBS.)

Magical Strings, *Islands Calling,* EarthBeat! Traveler, P.O. Box 1460, Redway, CA 95560-1460, 1-800-346-4445. E-mail:mlp@igc.apc.org.
This is soothing, lyrical harp music with an up tempo. The musical influences come from Ireland, Maui, the Bahamas, Jamaica, Africa and Madagascar.

Daniel Paul, *Rhythms of Paradise,* Soundings of the Planet, P.O. Box 43512, Tucson, AZ 85733, 1-800-93-PEACE.
Daniel Paul combines Indian melody and rhythm (on Indian Tabla drum and Tabla Tarong) with Celtic fiddle, African rhythm, Hawaiian influences

and other Western sensibilities. This is music for soft, gentle dancing with occasional deep journeys into hard-beat drumming.

Professor Trance and the Energizers, *Shaman's Breath,* Island Records, 825 Eighth Ave., New York, NY 10019.

This is "deep" dancing music—a combination of ancient drums with chanting and breath. Frank Natale (Prof. Trance) is also the author of *Trance Dance* (listed in the Bibliography) and the Natale Institute, where he leads workshops and trains instructors in trance dancing. As he says throughout this CD, "Our ancestors danced." By listening to this music, you get a feel for what they danced to.

Bill Whelan, *Riverdance,* Celtic Heartbeat, Atlantic Recording Corporation, 75 Rockefeller Plaza, New York, NY 10019, a Time Warner Company.

This is the soundtrack to the popular show which features Irish dance (now available on video). The vocal cuts don't inspire my dancing feet. But the instrumental pieces used for dancing are exquisite, from the lyrical and bold introduction, to the lament of the Uilleann (Irish bag) pipes to the fiery flamenco, "Firedance." There are Moorish and Russian influences as well. You don't have to do Irish dance to want to move to this foot-stomping music.

Willie and Lobo, *Fandango Nights,* Mesa Records. A division of Mesa/Bluemoon Recordings, Ltd. Distributed by Rhino Records, Inc.

Willie and Lobo are two American "rockin' gypsy" surfers living in Puerto Vallarta. Their original brand of Flamenco has tinges of Mexico, the Middle East and contains exquisite melodies that seem to have drifted straight off the ocean breeze. The title song is perhaps my all-time favorite up-beat dance song. But this whole CD has many dancing colors and moods.

When She Dances

When she dances
She shakes off her worldly disguise,
Leaves her shoes, worries and date book behind,
Slinks into velvet and spice
And lets her skin contain her gently,
Like a glove around her soul.

When she dances
She shuts down the outside,
Opens up the inside,
And clears away the static
So the dances simply come.

When she dances
She is traveling,
Back to the cliffs of Malta or Crete
Or the ring of Druid stones,
Or the caravan that finds a clearing,
Where the circle of dancing sisters
And the wide-hipped hug of the Earth
Rock her gently home.

When she dances,
She is fueled on fumes, stored for centuries

In the sealed up tombs of priestesses and queens.
Why their rage and sensual, throbbing majesty should come to life inside her
She does not know,
Except that it feels this way, when she dances.

When she dances, sometimes she is the future,
All gristle and lace
Hard angles meeting soft,
Logic and passion,
Flying at digital speed.

When she dances, sometimes the past melts away.
All that matters is this moment that seems to span all time.
Every step becomes a net, in which she captures her life,
Shines it up so others can see,
Then lets it go like a dream.

She has been consumed by so many dance styles,
Once hungered for steps and combinations
To put in her bag of tricks.
But she can't dance that way anymore,
Can't pray to the lines in the mirror,
Can't afford to fuss or worry and interrupt the flow.

It's true that often when she dances,
Every part of the story shows.
Her skin is thin as paper, the bruises yellow blue.
But other times when she dances,
Her story disappears.
She is anyone she wants to be when she dances.

When she doesn't dance,
And the days go by without celebration,
A crust forms.
She grows an edge and
Is impatient with others and herself.
But when she dances once again, she comes back to the temple.
The pressure drops to normal and she smiles.

Something else happens when she dances.
The stiffness in the morning dissipates in a steam.

The inelegance of gravity and age
Fade away . . .
Like magic.

When you look closely you cannot tell
If she is young, old or even middle-aged.
She is no particular age at all,
But the perpetual maiden,
In a mother's body,
With a wise woman's soul
She will let you see into
When she dances.

Selected Bibliography

Adrian, Marlene, and Cooper, John M. *Biomechanics of Human Movement*. Madison, Wis.: Brown and Benchmark, 1989.

Becker, Robert O., M.D., and Seldon, Gary. *The Body Electric, Electromagnetism and the Foundation of Life*. New York: Morrow, 1985.

Blair, Lawrence. *Rhythms of Vision, The Changing Patterns of Myth and Consciousness*. Dorset, Vt.: Destiny, 1991.

Bolen, Jean Shinoda, M.D. *Close to the Bone, Life-Threatening Illness and the Search for Meaning*. New York: Scribner, 1996.

———. *Goddesses in Every Woman*. New York: Harper & Row, 1985.

Borysenko, Joan, Ph.D. *A Woman's Book of Life, The Biology, Psychology and Spirituality of the Feminine Life Cycle*. New York: Riverhead, 1997.

Brennan, Barbara. *Light Emerging*. New York: Bantam, 1993.

Buonaventura, Wendy. *Serpent of the Nile, Women and Dance in the Arab World*. Brooklyn, NY: Interlink, 1989.

Carlton, Donna. *Looking for Little Egypt*. Bloomington, Indiana: IDD, 1994.

Chopra, Deepak. *Ageless Body, Timeless Mind*. New York: Harmony, 1993.

Croutier, Alev Lytle. *Harem, The World Beyond the Veil*. New York: Abbeville, 1989.

Doczi, George. *The Power of Limits, Proportional Harmonies in Nature, Art and Architecture*. Boston and London: Shambhala, 1994.

Douglas, Nik, and Slinger, Penny. *Sexual Secrets, The Alchemy of Ecstasy*. Rochester, Vt.: Destiny, 1979.

Duerk, Judith. *Circle of Stones, Woman's Journey to Herself*. San Diego: Lura-Media, 1989.

Edwards, Betty. *Drawing on the Right Side of the Brain.* New York: Tarcher/Putnam, 1988.

Fontana, David. *The Secret Language of Symbols, A Visual Key to Symbols and Their Meanings.* San Francisco: Chronicle, 1993.

Fraser, Laura. *Health* magazine, May/June, 1996.

Gadon, Elinor. *The Once and Future Goddess, A Sweeping Visual Chronicle of the Sacred Female and Her Reemergence in the Cultural Mythology of Our Time.* San Francisco: Harper, 1989.

Gilder, George. *Life after Television, The Coming Transformation of Media and American Life.* New York: Norton, 1994.

Gimbutas, Maria. *The Goddesses and Gods of Old Europe: Myths and Cult Images.* Berkeley: University of California Press, 1982.

Haskell, William L., Ph.D. "Resolving the Exercise Debate: More vs. Less." *Idea Today* magazine, San Diego: Oct. 1995.

Hopkins, Jerry. *Hula.* Hawaii: APA Productions, 1982.

Iglehart, Hallie. *Womanspirit: A Guide to Women's Wisdom.* San Francisco: Harper & Row, 1983.

Kerns, Deborah. "A Comparison of a Mind-Body Approach versus a Conventional Approach to Aerobic Dance." *Women's Health Digest. A Health Journal for Women* 7-1, New York: Jacob's Institute of Women's Health. Jan.–Feb., 1997.

Kingsley, David. *The Goddess' Mirror, Visions of the Divine from East and West.* New York: State University of New York Press, 1989.

Lawlor, Robert. *Sacred Geometry, Philosophy and Practice.* London: Thames and Hudson, 1982.

Lawson, Joan. *A History of Ballet and Its Makers.* London, Sir Isaac Pitman & Sons, 1964.

Leonard, Linda Schierse. *The Wounded Woman, Healing the Father-Daughter Relationship.* Boulder, Colo.: Shambhala Publications, 1991.

Mann, A.T., and Lyle, Jane. *Sacred Sexuality.* Dorset, England: Element Books, 1995.

Mishkin, Julie Russo, and Schill, Marta. *The Complete Belly Dancer.* New York: Doubleday, 1973.

Monaghan, Patricia. *The Book of Goddesses and Heroines.* St. Paul, Minn.: Llewellyn Publications, 1993.

Murdock, Maureen. *The Heroine's Journey, Woman's Quest for Wholeness.* Boston, Mass.: Shambhala Publications, 1990.

Natale, Frank. *Trance Dance, The Dance of Life.* Dorset, England: Element Books, 1995.

Nieuwkerk, Karen Van. *A Trade Like Any Other, Female Singers and Dancers in Egypt.* Austin, Tex.: University of Texas Press, 1995.

Noble, Vicki. *Motherpeace. A Way to the Goddess through Myth, Art and the Tarot.* San Francisco: Harper, 1983.

Pollock, Rachel. *Seventy-eight Degrees of Wisdom, A Book of Tarot*, Part One, The Major Arcana. London/San Francisco: Thorsons, HarperCollins, 1980.

Purce, Jill. *The Mystic Spiral, Journey of the Soul.* New York: Thames and Hudson, 1974.

Reed, William. *Ki, A Practical Guide for Westerners.* Tokyo and New York: Japan Publications, 1986.

Schneider, Michael. *A Beginner's Guide to Constructing the Universe, A Voyage From 1 to 10.* New York: HarperCollins, 1994.

Sheehy, Gail. *New Passages, Mapping Your Life across Time.* New York: Random House, 1995.

Starhawk. *Dreaming the Dark.* Boston: Beacon Press, 1982.

———. *The Spiral Dance: A Rebirth of the Ancient Religion of the Great Goddess.* San Francisco: Harper & Row, 1979.

Stewart, R. J. *Celtic Gods, Celtic Goddesses.* London: Blandford, 1990.

Tansley, David. *Subtle Body, Essence and Shadow.* New York: Thames and Hudson, 1994.

Walker, Barbara G. *The Women's Encyclopedia of Myths and Secrets.* San Francisco: Harper, 1983.

Wosien, Maria-Gabriele. *Sacred Dance, Encounter with Gods.* New York: Avon, 1974.

Index

About the Author

Karen Andes is the author of *A Woman's Book of Strength*, a producer of award-winning videos, a lecturer, teacher and trainer, particularly in the field of women's fitness in body, spirit and mind. She has served as the Women's Health Advisor for Interactive Marketing Ventures in Wayne, Pennsylvania, and is a former co-owner of Gold's Gym in Marin, California. She has traveled extensively training fitness instructors and is a five-star presenter with IDEA (the International Association of Fitness Professionals). Ms. Andes lives with her husband in San Rafael, California.

To Contact Karen Andes

To find out more information about Karen's . . .

- videotapes and audiotapes

- workshops and classes

- public-speaking engagements and convention appearances or to include her in your next event, visit the Web site at: http://www.world-dancer.com

Karen is also available as a producer or consultant for other video productions—instructional, music or documentary.

Send E-mail to kandes@worlddancer.com
Send letters to Karen Andes, c/o Perigee Books
200 Madison Ave., 16th Floor
NY, NY 10016.